Leadership in Business

Raju Khatri

authorHOUSE®

AuthorHouse™
1663 Liberty Drive
Bloomington, IN 47403
www.authorhouse.com
Phone: 1-800-839-8640

© 2012 Raju Khatri. All rights reserved.

No part of this book may be reproduced, stored in a retrieval system, or transmitted by any means without the written permission of the author.

Published by AuthorHouse 07/08/2012

ISBN: 978-1-4772-1098-7 (sc)
ISBN: 978-1-4772-1097-0 (hc)
ISBN: 978-1-4772-1096-3 (e)

Library of Congress Control Number: 2012909193

Any people depicted in stock imagery provided by Thinkstock are models, and such images are being used for illustrative purposes only. Certain stock imagery © Thinkstock.

This book is printed on acid-free paper.

Because of the dynamic nature of the Internet, any web addresses or links contained in this book may have changed since publication and may no longer be valid. The views expressed in this work are solely those of the author and do not necessarily reflect the views of the publisher, and the publisher hereby disclaims any responsibility for them.

Raju Khatri is a practiced young entrepreneur, trainer, and motivator as well as world vice president of JCI (Junior Chamber International). JCI is an international organization focused on individual development, especially dealing with leadership and entrepreneurship through training, seminars, and practical experience in 116 countries with more than 6,000 communities. His life goal is to share knowledge with youth in order to assist them to achieve success in their present situations. After delivering thousands and thousands of motivational speeches, this practiced international trainer now finds it appropriate to share his knowledge through the pen.

Raju believes a book's purpose is not to demonstrate the skills of the author. Rather, it should be motivated by sharing interesting, ultimate knowledge with others. This book's leadership in business is a combination of creation and collection, where readers can get the motivation and logical points toward starting or running a business.

Contents

Chapter 1	**Why We Fail Even Fulfilled Duty**	**1**
	Introduction	2
	Sense and Its Relation to Business	2
	Smart Work Rather than Hard Work	3
	Activated and Idle Brains	3
	How to Utilize the Brain	4
	How to Become a Positive Thinker?	9
	How to Utilize the Mind According to Hinduism	14
	Who Will Win the World?	20
Chapter 2	**Advice for a Young Businessperson**	**23**
	Business and Publicity	27
	Motivate Yourself—"If He Can Do Business, I Can Too"	31
	Start Your Business Simply, and Hand It Over as a Memory	32
	Don't Crow Like a Hen; Work Like a Man	33
	Be an Ant's Head Rather than an Elephant's Tail	33
	Regard Yourself as a Leader, Not a Laborer	34
	Realize Yourself—Everything Is Possible, But Nothing Is Guaranteed	34
Chapter 3	**Who Can Become a Businessperson?**	**39**
	People Who Have No Money	42
	People Who Have No Time	48
	People Who Never Work	50
Chapter 4	**Career Plan in Business**	**53**
	Differences in Manners Between a Normal Man and a Businessman	54
	Six Floors in the Business Pyramid of	58
Chapter 5	**Turn your Behavior into Business Behavior**	**69**
	Take Over If You Are Perfect; Hand Over If You Are Not Perfect	72

	Invest Others' Money	73
	invest; Do Not Spend	74
	Aim to Be an Entrepreneur, Not a Millionaire	74
	Don't Push Sales; Allow Customers to Buy	75
	Follow the Traditional Traits of Entrepreneurship (Smiling, Dedication, Time Management, and Sacrifice)	76
	Never Be Nervous; Be Spiritual	77
Chapter 6	**The Destination of Business**	**81**
	The Earning Cycle	82
Chapter 7	**Leadership in Business**	**87**
	The Business Family	89
	The Investor	89
	Situational Leadership	91
	Workers	96
	Customers	101
	Leadership Ideas from an Ancient Era	105
	Conclusion About Leadership	118
Chapter 8	**Formula for Success**	**121**
	The Four P's: Planning, Preparation, Practice, and Presentation	122
	Enemies of Business	132
	Conclusion	134
	Knowledge Is Not a Power	134

CHAPTER ONE

Why We Fail Even Fulfilled Duty

One evening, Ramesh was drinking, as usual. Wine stimulates one, heats up the mind, and makes the body stagger. This happened to Ramesh.

His house was across the lake, a half-hour trip. Still drunk, Ramesh decided to go home. He found a boat and sat in it, heading exactly toward the house. He rowed and rowed but made no progress. Why?

Only in the morning, as daybreak ruled out the dark night and Ramesh got rid of the effect of wine, he came back to his senses. He looked around him and discovered that he hadn't untied the rope of the boat. He had rowed and worked with no results. It was the reason he was where he had been.

There are youths today who have studied much and invested in business much but realize that they haven't been successful in their lives. They say that they have carried out their duty without any fault but haven't achieved the goal. Why? The cause is lack of proper awareness. The man was not adequately aware and senseful, and as a result, he forgot to untie the anchor.

Introduction

Here is a term: "leadership in business." It's a combination of two different words—*leadership*, the ability to lead others; and *business*, today's most burning issue on the economic planet. A person who coordinates leadership and business in a meaningful way will be able to compete successfully in today's world. Let's start the analysis of experience that will really find the root point to help achieve more business success.

Sense and Its Relation to Business

For leadership in business or any competitive field, perfect activity of the brain is the most powerful wining factor. People says that "practice makes man perfect" but it is not true at all. Suppose a man open a small shop and run for many years, it is a kind of practice but him still running same business in same position. If practice makes man prefect he should had great business at later days, but he might not be, so we say "A perfect practice (use of brain) only makes business perfect." We human beings have two types of abilities—physical and mental. Mental power is more important and decisive than physical power. An obvious example is that a man is quite small in size relative to an elephant, but he is able to ride upon it and guide it. The physical size of the elephant doesn't affect man in this regard, as it is all decided by the brain. This is the world of "mind sale," and whoever sells his mind effectively will be able to achieve his goals and success in life.

People frequently can manage time, business, and families very well, but mind management is a very difficult job.

> *In Mahabharata, the ancient holy book of*
> *Hinduism, when Arjun, the hero of the epic,*
> *was afflicted by illness, he said to Krishna,*
> *"Mind is very restless, forceful and strong.*
> *O Krishna, Krishna! it is more difficult to*
> *control the mind than the wind."*

In this way, it is obvious that ordinary people may find it difficult to manage their minds properly. Business is a kind of chase game, where lots of ideas should be created. These ideas come from the mind, if the mind is fresh. So here in the beginning of the book, I would like to start mind management through modern logic and ancient religious logic. Such mind management is at the core of successful leadership in business.

Smart Work Rather than Hard Work

Many people use the bell of an alarm clock to wake them up in the morning. They set it as they like. Most people, including youths and their parents, are either busy in their work or job or they have entertainment the whole day long. They may not care what time they go to bed, and when they do, it is often quite late. They fall into deep slumber due to their exhaustion. In the early morning, they are interrupted by the alarm clock. It irritates them, but they are obliged to get up without sufficient sleep. They are still drowsy, but they have duty. They aren't in a fresh mood. A man needs at least eight hours' sleep a day according to research. If you go to your work with insufficient sleep or rest, it can easily be imagined how you will (not) accomplish your work.

What is required is for you to go to bed for eight hours. If you go to bed at eight o'clock in the evening, you can easily get up at four o'clock in the morning. Now you will have sufficient sleep, you won't require an alarm clock, you will get up at the right time by yourself, and you will always be fresh in your too. Both the use of the alarm and sleeping at the right time aim at achieving the same goal and both are duties, but which is more effective is clear.

Look at nature, which teems with a lot of creations. A human being is one of them and the best of all. We humans are different from animals mainly in the sense that animals do not think of others whereas humans do. We humans have different brain composition and life structures in comparison with the animals. Humans are humans chiefly by the possession of human brains. So let's see how we can activate our brains smartly.

Activated and Idle Brains

In my society, a man fathered two sons. In the course of time, the sons grew up, and the father equally divided his belongings

> between his sons. Later, one of the sons may be a prosperous and successful person, while the other may go bankrupt. One may become a doctor; the other may be addicted to drugs. This differing behavior is the consequence of how they activated their brains. The first one activated and utilized his brain and thus became a doctor, whereas the other one either stayed idle or misused his brain and became a druggie. Not all the things perceived with the eyes are always true. What we need is to analyze the perceived data in our brain by activating the brain.

The world-famous blind woman Helen Keller has mentioned that "the knowledge not recognized by the mind is more dangerous than the blind eyes themselves."

We can easily sum up this idea by saying that the success of a person depends on how much he or she activates the brain.

How to Utilize the Brain

Mind refresher: *A customer in a restaurant: "How long do you expect me to wait for half a chicken?"*

Waiter: "Until someone else orders the other half. We can't just go and kill half a hen!"

Utilizing brains means using sense, and using sense means being aware. Sometimes people say, "You are senseless," but it is not true. Almost everyone exercises their sense. Think of how many hairs a man has on his head and body. Millions and millions of them, so that they are not even countable! But if somebody touches just one of the hairs on the head, the person certainly has feeling of the event. So you may imagine this is how you are in your sense.

There are several ways to utilize the brain in order to use your senses. Here are some ways to help you utilize yours.

Avoid hasty decisions.

We all have mouths with our articulators in ready positions, so it is very easy to verbalize our thoughts.

Word has great power.
  It can murder.
  It can save.
  It can accept.
  It can reject.
  So

  Think twice before vocalizing.

It is always better for us to think twice before we speak. If we utter our words without any contemplation, it is more or less similar to a blind person targeting a goal post. Hasty decisions are likely to bring unexpected consequences. There is no brain activity in prompt decision.

Think of the 'W's on each matter—why, what, when, where, who, whom—and only then shape your perspective.

Newton was sitting under an apple tree. In our daily life, if an apple falls down from the tree, what do we do? The answer is obvious—say thanks to God and eat that fruit. But Newton was curious about why the apple fell down, why it didn't go up or left or right. It was the base on which he founded the law of gravity. The letter W structure is up and down. Using this W in every matter may activate your brain up and down.

Analyze the positive and negative impacts of each issue.

Ask yourself questions about the impacts when making a decision. By using some analysis of potential outcomes, you can make smarter decisions.

<u>Negative impact</u>	<u>Positive impact</u>
Do we need hard work?	Do we need smart work?
Do we have time difficulty?	Are we enjoying the time?
May we get the profit?	May we reach the target?
Become lazy.	Motivate further.

| Like to quit the job. | Promote the job further. |

In your analysis, positive impacts should be more important than negative ones.

Analyze the matter from different points of view.

Any matter or issue can be viewed from different points of view. Each of your activities may have lots of aspects, and you can analyze them from different perspectives. If you analyze the episodes from only one perspective, you may not approach the truth and reality.

Enjoy your work.

If somebody is seen sleeping, he or she is generally asked to get up and go to work. That is not a good thing to do because sleeping is also a very important and essential work. Almost *all activities are works. Only useless activities may not be categorized as works.*

I know a little about army culture: If there is no job to be done, the commander may order his orderlies to dig holes or tunnels, which may not be required at the time, and later he may order them again to fill the dug holes or tunnels. That is not any work at all. If we want to enjoy our lives, we need to enjoy the activities we perform in our daily life, all except the ones that we subconsciously or unconsciously perform in our dreams.

A very cheerful father, Arbindo, said:

> *When we are eating, let us enjoy our meals.*
> *When we are in a playground, let us enjoy our games.*
> *When we are in our school, let us enjoy study.*
> *When we are in bed, let us enjoy our sleep.*
> *When in the toilet, let us enjoy defecation.*
> *When in difficulty, let us enjoy optimism.*

Mind refresher: *"Money is not the origin of happiness. A man with 50 million rupees is not necessarily more happy than a man with 49 million rupees."*

Entertain yourself with intelligence games
like chess, puzzles, and so on.

Whether it is a machine or an animal or a human body, it requires good exercise for proper maintenance. To keep the body in accurate condition, physical exercise is required. As far as mental health is concerned, intelligence games like chess and puzzles may maintain the brains properly. A frequently activated brain will work properly at the time of hardship in a person's life.

Practice yoga and meditation.

No doubt! Meditation maintains the consciousness, and consciousness is the power of a fresh brain. Meditation is very helpful in activating the brain.

Load your mind with positive thoughts.

Garbage in a room never gives perfume. Similarly we can easily understand that if a mind is filled with negative thoughts, it is like garbage and is primarily harmful to oneself.

The famous psychiatrist Dr. David R. Hawkins, who is a prominent scientist of kinesiology (the study of the principles of mechanics and anatomy in relation to human movement), quantified his ideas about the power of positive thinking versus negative thinking. By using certain muscle-testing techniques, kinesiological research has determined that certain systems of thought are actually more powerful than others in promoting the health and well-being of living creatures.

Scientists have individuals speak various statements as the reactions of their muscles are monitored. Through the observation of the muscles' reactions, scientists can determine if a statement evokes a positive reaction in the muscles or not. This science of the body has been shown to be useful in determining the actual power of some statements as opposed to others.

The research is extremely beneficial to those who examine the findings, and even more studies are continuing today.

Scientists have gone even further than the simple testing of statements to determine if they are powerful or not. They have devised a scale of measurement that can actually determine the level of power for individual statements, and they have used the reaction of the muscles to determine those levels according to the science of kinesiology. As an example, a scale of power was set up from zero to 1000; test subjects were told that zero represented absolutely no power, while 1000 represented the most power possible for a human being to acquire. The scale was set up as a logarithmic scale, so that the number 2 was actually representative of x to the second power, indicating a much larger jump in power than might first be indicated by the numbers. Individual statements were then spoken, and it was suggested that each statement carried a certain level of power with it.

The muscles of the test subjects were seen to react in kinesiological research such that the findings have been quite astonishing. In fact, many individual words were proven again and again to have more power than other words, such as in the case of the word "anger," which consistently tested at a level of 150 among thousands of test subjects. Similarly, the word "fear" was tested by scientists to hold a very low power level of only 100. Among the lowest levels of power were certain words such as "guilt," which held a power level of only 30, and "shame," which held an extremely low level of power at only 20.

In terms of the power of positive thought, there have been many words that were reported to score very high on the measuring scale. The word "love" consistently scored extremely high at 500, and the word "peace" was scored at 600. It is clear from these findings that there is an inherent power to positive thinking that can actually have a physical effect on your body if the word is repeated and made to become part of your lifestyle.

These findings—which are reported at length on the website http://www.positivethinkingnow.com/category/positive-thoughts—suggest a number of things, all of which have become part of a very extensive research project headed up by Hawkins, who has already been celebrated with numerous awards for his work. Among one of the most significant implications of this work is the fact that nothing is thought to have come about as a result of an accident or a "random" occurrence. With the discovery that everything carries with it a certain level of power, it is also the case that nothing can be said to be part of an accident. Individual people themselves can also be tested as to be holding a certain amount of energy or "power," and their names can be spoken such that the reactions of the muscles can also be tested. With this comes the obvious conclusion that, not only certain thoughts, but everything that is capable of being held in mind is subject to a certain test of power.

The future holds many bright possibilities for the progress of our own well-being, and science is now at the cutting edge of helping us to increase our healthy minds and our lifestyles in a monumental way. It is only a matter of time before the power of positive thinking can become an intimate part of your life if you choose to align yourself with it.

How to Become a Positive Thinker?

(Much of the information in this section comes from the website http://www.positivethinkingnow.com/what-is-positive-thought/21/.)

What one person thinks is positive, another person may think is negative; but people are often mistaken, and there must be a way of determining what is really positive and what is really negative in life. What is that method that determines a positive thought from a negative thought? Hawkins has proposed the idea that some thoughts are detrimental to our general health as human beings and others tend to promote health and life in all living beings.

In his book *Power vs. Force*, Dr. Hawkins explains how some thoughts are accompanied by a positive energy field, which brings about more power in our lives. Other thoughts carry a negative energy field and rely on the negative requirement of force to have any effect. Although many negative thoughts are indicative of the use of force, these thoughts do not tend to sustain our lives as a general rule; instead, they tend to lead toward the debilitating emotions of anger, fear, and grief. On a calibrated scale of energy, Dr. Hawkins has placed many different thoughts at different levels of power. Thoughts of shame or guilt are the least productive thoughts that we possess, as are thoughts indicative of apathy and grief. Although we may occasionally find ourselves thinking and feeling in terms of guilt or apathy, these emotions are far from being positive and actually can lead to suicide and death in their most extreme forms. In order to cultivate more positive thoughts, we are encouraged by Dr. Hawkins to let go of these negative mind states and to integrate more positive states of being into our lives.

One of the first kinds of positive thought that people can employ in their lives is courage. Although we all experience fear, we are encouraged through various practices to give up our fears and to embrace a more courageous attitude toward life. Many spiritual practices teach us that fear is actually an illusion that the majority of human beings are trapped under. We fear our own death at every turn, as well as rejection, failure, and any number of "negative" outcomes in life. The reality of this, however, is that our fear is actually the thing that creates these outcomes more than anything else. Rather than feeding our fears by constantly engaging in fearful thoughts and emotions, we can turn to courage as a way out of our problems.

Another of the greatest and most positive thought patterns is willingness. When we employ the willingness to pursue our own self-examination and betterment, we encourage more positive thoughts to come into our lives. Put on a happy face even when it doesn't feel so easy and practice kindness to the people around you. This act of willingness each day will help to promote a positive energy in your head and will eventually turn your thoughts toward more positive ones. It's a simple practice that can work wonders in your life.

Finally, the two greatest means to a more positive pattern of thinking are to pursue the goals of love and peace in your life. Acting in a loving way toward the people around you requires a great amount of energy and is actually something that many people recoil from in fear. It is actually an incredibly unnatural effort for many people to pursue love, but this is part of the proof that this energy is extremely powerful and can transform your thoughts into a more positive direction almost overnight.

In addition to love, there is energy even greater than love, which is actually the source of all positive thinking itself. That energy is the energy of peace. A peaceful state of mind is something that is almost unheard of in our modern day. How often do you actually sit still and feel that your thoughts and emotions are completely at peace? You may be hard-pressed to admit that this rarely even happens when you are sleeping, because peace is often only achieved by the greatest practitioners of advanced yoga and meditative techniques. Many students have spent years pursuing the state of being wherein their minds are completely at peace and can remain in that state for extended periods of time. Indeed, peace is truly the highest level of positive thought that can be attained.

Next time you are arguing with someone over what is positive and what is negative, think again. Arguing is rarely a positive thought, and it isn't your logic or your reason that will ultimately solve this dispute. Turning your life toward love and peace is the ultimate positive thought you can have; it is something that everyone could benefit from if they were to truly put their minds to this task.

Use affirmation power.

(Much of the information in this section comes from the website http://www.successconsciousness.com/index_00000a.htm.)

Affirmations are positive statements that describe a desired situation and are repeated many times in order to impress the subconscious mind and trigger it into positive action. In order to ensure the effectiveness of the affirmations, they have to be repeated with attention, conviction, interest, and desire.

Imagine that you are swimming with your friends in a pool. They swim fifteen rounds, something you have never done before, and as you want to win their respect, you want to show them that you can do it too. You start swimming, and at the same time keep repeating in your mind, "I can do it, I can do it …" You keep thinking and believing that you are going to complete the fifteen rounds. What are you actually doing? You are repeating positive affirmations.

Most people repeat in their minds negative words and statements concerning the situations and events in their lives, and consequently, create undesirable situations. Words and statements work both ways—to build or destroy. It is the way we use them that determines whether they are going to bring good or harmful results.

Often, people repeat negative statements in their minds, without even being aware of what they are doing. Do you keep thinking and telling yourself that you cannot do something, you are too lazy, you lack inner strength, or you are going to fail? Your subconscious mind accepts as true what you keep saying, and eventually attracts corresponding events and situations into your life, regardless of whether they are good or bad for you, so why not choose only positive statements?

Affirmations program the mind in the same way that commands and scripts program a computer. They work in the same manner as creative visualization. The repeated words help you focus your mind on your aim, and automatically build corresponding mental images in the conscious mind, which affect the subconscious mind. The conscious mind, the mind you think with, starts this process, and then the subconscious mind takes charge. By using this process consciously and intently, you can affect your subconscious mind and thereby transform your habits, behavior, mental attitude, and reactions, and even reshape your external life.

Sometimes results appear quickly, but often more time is required. Depending on your goal, sometimes you might attain immediate results, and sometimes it might take days, weeks, months, or more. Getting results depends on several factors, such as the time, focus, faith, and feelings you invest in repeating your affirmations, on the strength of your desire, and on how big or small your goal is.

It is important to understand that repeating positive affirmations for a few minutes and then thinking negatively the rest of the day neutralizes the effects of the positive words. You have to refuse to think negative thoughts if you wish to attain positive results.

Repeat affirmations for effect.

It is advisable to repeat affirmations that are not too long as they are easier to remember. Repeat them every time your mind is not engaged in something important, such as while traveling in a bus or a train, waiting in line, walking, and so on, but do not affirm while driving or crossing a street. You may also repeat them in special sessions of five to ten minutes each several times a day.

Relax any physical, emotional, or mental tension while affirming. The stronger the concentration, the more faith you have in what you are doing, the more feelings you put into the act, the stronger and faster will be the results.

Choose only positive words, describing what you really want. If you desire to lose weight, do not tell yourself "I am not fat" or "I am losing weight." These are negative statements, bringing into the mind mental images of what you do not want. Say instead, "I am getting slim" or "I have reached my right weight." Such words evoke positive images in the mind.

Always affirm in the present tense, not the future tense. Saying, "I will be rich," means that you intend to be rich one day in the indefinite future, but not now. It is more effective to say and also feel, "I am rich now," and the subconscious mind will work overtime to make this happen now, in the present.

The power of affirmations can help you to transform your life. By stating what you want to be true in your life, you mentally and emotionally see and feel it as true, regardless of your current circumstances, and thereby attract it into your life.

Some Examples of Positive Affirmations

- I am well and happy.
- Wealth is pouring into my life.
- I am sailing on the river of wealth.
- I am getting wealthier each day.
- My body is healthy and functioning in a very good way.
- I have a lot of energy.
- I study and comprehend quickly.
- My mind is calm.
- I am calm and relaxed in every situation.
- My thoughts are under my control.
- I radiate love and happiness.

- I am surrounded by love.
- I have a perfect job for me.
- I am living in the house of my dreams.
- I have good and loving relations with my wife or husband.
- I have a wonderful and satisfying job.
- I have the means to travel abroad whenever I want to.
- I am successful in whatever I do.
- Everything is getting better every day.

How to Utilize the Mind According to Hinduism

Our world depends on two fundamentals: God-made and man-made. In other words, God and man are the two powers in the world. We have been in search of ancient books on how to beautify the modern world and there has been research in this regard, but almost all the philosophers in the world agree that the Vedas are the oldest holy book in the world. They were written about three thousand years ago. Unfortunately people are ignoring such important, holy, and sacred books about human lives.

There are two views about the Vedas. One of them argues that the Vedas contain eternal knowledge and they are the only books to study. This view also argues that they are the blessings of God.

The other view states that the Vedas are scientific in their sense and therefore they contain superior knowledge. Such superior knowledge is open for all, but the conservative, traditional people who regard themselves as the saviors of the holy book are preventing others from reading or listening to the Vedas. Such people regard the books as only belonging to them, but if the Vedas contain knowledge for all human beings, they need to be open for all. It is apparent that there are many facts and much scientific knowledge in the Vedas, but as they have been kept from many people, the facts and the knowledge have been hidden to a great extent. The Vedas themselves express that knowledge is endless and it can be transmitted from one person to another person. Therefore, I am trying to reveal some of the facts of the Vedas in this book so that common people will understand this knowledge to some extent. There are four episodes in the Vedas:

- Rigveda gives knowledge about truth and the deeds of human beings.
- Samaveda tells us about worship and yoga philosophy.
- Atharveda tells about medicines and God.
- Yajurveda states that mind is the inner flame of knowledge.

The Yajurveda Mantra says that God is everywhere, almighty, all-knowing, formless without any nervous system, purest, away from sins, away to face any result of any karmas (deeds), and knows every soul. It further states that nobody has made God but God creates the universe, has given the eternal knowledge of the four Vedas, and always gives said knowledge at the beginning of every universe to know the science and deeds of all concerns. According to the Vedas, God first revealed the truth and the knowledge to four saints (Rishimunis), and in turn the knowledge was imparted to their disciples, who were the great personalities (Rama, Krishna, Arjun, etc.) in the past. Eventually the same knowledge was transmitted to common human beings in the course of time.

If a baby is brought up in a forest, out of the community, he will certainly not gain any knowledge. Miranda, Prospero's daughter in Shakespeare's play *The Tempest,* is an example of this kind. She was born in the palace but was brought up on an uninhabited island by the father and thus was an untrained and naïve girl. There is an unanswered question: where did knowledge first come from? The Vedas say that God is the source of knowledge. First He gave knowledge to the four Rishis. Rishi patanjali in yoga shastra sutra 1/26 says the same thing—God is the first guru of the four Rishis.

We all are the children of God. Our parents are only the creators of our outer body. The outer body is only the shape that is all controlled by the inner body that is the "self" or the "soul." In reality, we are the soul. Our body is only the temporary being. The Vedas say that the body dies but not the soul. It is all controlled by God, who may grant a reincarnation to a human again and again. The lust for property and other comforts are all for the outer body, whereas the soul is connected with the power of thought. The Vedas focus on the fact that we need to do true deeds per the guidance of the Vedas to win salvation in our lives. We can sit for penance and then listen to the preaching of the gurus; eventually we may be able to control the senses in order to prevent ourselves from addiction and we can get involved in good deeds, help the poor, and learn knowledge.

The fundamentals in the Vedas in brief are:

1. The pious deeds that give fruitful results and the happiest life while alive and also after the death of body are called *religion*, the soul being immortal.

2. There are three immortal matters that haven't been made by anyone—God, souls, and nature. God and souls are alive, whereas nature isn't.

3. As a man makes a house from live human sources and nonalive materials, God needs nonalive nature to create the universe, which is destructible.

4. We are souls, but not the body. We live in the body.

5. The body gets destroyed, but not the soul.

6. According to the deeds, a soul gets reincarnated under the control of God.

7. The whole articles of the world—money, assets, food, even the body, sun, moon, and so on—are meant for our body, and our body is meant for our soul. By doing pious deeds according to the Vedas, including worship (Yajna, yoga practice, etc.), one can get salvation.

8. *Tapasya* means listening to vedic preaching or any good preaching, to control our five senses, five perceptions, and mind, not to think bad, to do holy *Yagya*, to donate to right and needy people, to attain peace, and to study the Vedas.

9. Human beings must progress simultaneously in both ways, that is, in science and universal progress and in spiritualism, because one-sided progress is totally harmful to human beings.

There are many fundamentals in the Vedas, such as duties of students, family holders, *Vanprasthis* or *sanyasis*, mothers, fathers, and so on. It is not out of place to mention that the Vedas only contain fundamentals and not any kind of story.

Many topics of science are in Vedic philosophy. For example, the earth moves around the sun. Very few know that this is already mentioned in the Yajurveda mantra and that many science topics are covered in the Vedas.

Present science says that there are about two hundred matters or elements, whereas Rigveda says there are 720. Modern doctors say to drink boiled water, which has been prescribed by Atharvaveda in its beginning mantras. So many such secrets are revealed in the Vedas. The knowledge of the Vedas in my view is very useful when we make our attempt to have our mind management in a proper way. Any knowledge without vedic knowledge may be incomplete. The Vedas are not difficult, because the Vedas are to be listened to first and not to be read. Listening is not difficult.

> *"A healthy mind has a healthy body." The mental health of the individual plays a significant role in the well-being of a person. The WHO (World Health Organization) defines health as "physical, mental and social 'well-being.'" During the past two decades, interest and research in the field of mental health and mental disorders have grown rapidly. A recent study conducted by WHO (see http://www.ncbi.nlm.nih.gov/pmc/articles/PMC2962283/pdf/IJPsy-41-5.pdf) predicted that in terms of disease burden, by the year 2020 depressive illness will become the number-two disease in the world, overriding diabetes, cancer, arthritis, and so on. Depressive disease is universal and has been prevalent in the society since time immemorial.*

The Vedic View of Mind

(Much of the information in this section comes from http://www.ncbi.nlm.nih.gov/pmc/articles/PMC2962283/pdf/IJPsy-41-5.pdf.)

Mind has been conceived to be a functional element of ATMAN (soul, which is self) in the Vedas, which are the earliest written script of the human race. In Rigveda and Yajurveda, there is mention of prayer through mantras for noble thoughts to come in the mind. It is mentioned that thoughts determine and influence facial appearance and thoughts can be purified through mantras and purified thoughts influence instincts. In the Vedas, there is emphasis on prevention of mental pain (depression).

In Rigveda, the speed of mind, curiosity for methods of mental happiness, prayers for mental happiness, and methods of increasing medha (intelligence) have been described. It is further stated in Rigveda that purification of mind prevents diseases in human beings and therefore one should have noble thoughts. The power of mind in healing has also been described. First time the three traits of personality—sattva (good character), rajas (medium character) and tamas (bad character)—were described, and also mental illnesses were independently identified along with physical illnesses where it has been prayed that these mental illnesses may not destroy this body. In Yajurveda the mind has been conceptualized as the inner flame of knowledge. It describes perceiving knowledge as mind, mind is described as yoga, and Samadhi (state of mind) as all our sensory organs are under control of the mind.

According to the Bhagabad Gita, the senses and the objects constantly blast the mind. It is said that the self is like the lord of the chariot and the body is his chariot. The intellect is the charioteer and the mind the reins. The senses, they say, are the horses; the objects of the senses are the roads. The senses (horses) are to be controlled by the buddhi (the charioteers) through the reins, the mind. The mind restrained or unrestrained by the buddhi leads to the region of vivid joy or the cycle of birth and rebirth (samsara), respectively. The mind of man is like a veritable battlefield—*Ranahkshetra*—in which there is an endless state of war between opposing forces. This constant tussle within the mind is called *psychomacia* by the ancient Greeks.

Ayurveda derives its roots from *Atharvaveda*, and it is one of the ancient sciences, meaning science of life. The classic written documents are Charak Samhita and Shushrut Samhita. These two describe mental disorders and personality types according to trigunas (the sattva, raja, and tama) and tridoshas—the three humors (faults) in the body (vat, pitta, kapha). The following causative factors are mentioned for disorders:

1. Pragyaparadh: Involvement in socially unsanctioned behavior and involvement in actions arising out of envy, pride, fear, anger, greed, attraction, and proud and deluded thinking.

2. Anuchit brahmacharya: One who is following the rules of brahmacharya, which includes Indriya Nigrah, that is, control over the demands of the instincts. Due to this, when the person carries out activities to gratify his instinctual needs, his conscience is not able to control his mind and becomes conflict-ridden, which leads to mental disorders like depression.

3. Durbal satva: People who have weak satva characteristics have increased raja and tama characteristics, which lead to emotions like anger, and uncontrolled emotions, which lead to mental disorders.

4. Durbal Sharir: Nutritional deficiencies leading to weak physical structures can lead to mental disorders.

5. Sharir dosh vikriti: According to Sushrut and Charak, increase in one of the three humors of the body—either vat, pitta, or kapha—leads to mental disturbances like insomnia, anger, fear, and so on.

The above excerpts from the Vedas clarify that there are both aspects in the mind—good and bad. We are required to get rid of the bad aspects of the mind and go ahead in its management if we are to be on our path of achieving success.

Who Will Win the World?

The term "business" is like "busyness" —busy + ness. In other words, business means remaining busy on a job. A painter always goes on painting even after he has already made his best one; a record breaker always heads for more and better records even after he has already been in the *Guinness Book of World Records*. Likewise, a businessman, no matter how much he earns, goes on earning and earning. There is not any limitation of satisfaction and gratification. Each matter or object in the world has monetary value, and therefore a businessperson is always attempting to earn as much as he can.

All men in the world may have different professions, but all professions have three common targets, that is, the three P's—penny, popularity, and prestige. A doctor expects the same rewards from his service; a politician has the same interests in his job; then why not a business personality? Sometimes we find a very popular person undergoing some difficulty due to lack of money. Sometimes we see a very rich person content of his money, but he may be craving popularity. Individual development is usually linked with the desire for the obtainment of the above-mentioned things—penny, popularity, and prestige. A business is not only for money; it is carried out for honor and popularity too. Let's see an example of this kind.

Whoever has earned the most or owns the most property is regarded as a successful entrepreneur. Leadership in business is based on the power of thinking, innovating, and planning.

Case Study
(from http://en.wikipedia.org/wiki/Masaru_Ibuka)

Japanese business leader **Masaru Ibuka** *was born in a normal family background. After graduating, he went to work at Photo-Chemical Laboratory, a company that processed movie film. In 1945, he left the company and founded a radio repair shop in Tokyo. Starting from a small radio repair shop, he became a worldwide famous name as Sony.*

As of this printing, Revenue *US$ 86.64 billion,* Operating income *US$ 2.41 billion,* Net income *US$ 2.96 billion,* Total assets *US$ 155.94 billion, with 168,200 employees.*

His honors and awards include:

- *1960, Awarded* Medal of Honor with Blue Ribbon *from H.M. the Emperor of Japan*
- *1978, Decorated by H.M. the Emperor of Japan, with the First Class Order of the Sacred Treasures*
- *1986, Decorated by H.M. the Emperor of Japan, with the First Class Order of the Rising Sun with the Grand Cordon*
- *1986, Decorated by H.M. the King of Sweden, with Commander First Class of the* Royal Order of the Polar Star
- *1992, Decorated by H.M. the Emperor of Japan, with* Order of Culture
- *1964, Received Distinguished Services Award from the Institute of Electrical Communication Engineers of Japan*
- *1972, Received* IEEE Founders Medal *from the* Institute of Electrical and Electronics Engineers
- *1976, Honorary Doctor of Engineering,* Sophia University, *Tokyo*
- *1979, Honorary Doctor of Science,* Waseda University, *Tokyo*
- *1981, Received Humanism and Technology Award from the Aspen Institute for Humanistic Studies*
- *1986, Awarded* Eduard Rhein Ring of Honor, *German* Eduard Rhein Foundation
- *1989, Designated Person of Cultural Merits by* Ministry of Education
- *1990,* IEEE *Masaru Ibuka Consumer Electronics Award named in his honor*
- *1991, Received the Presidential Award and Medallion from the* University of Illinois *(USA)*

CHAPTER TWO

ADVICE FOR A YOUNG BUSINESSPERSON

I was in Singapore once returning from Japan in the course of my Jaycee mission. My Singaporean friend asked me to visit Singapore for a Jaycees program.

I observed that they have a different way of operating programs and seminars. In Nepal, we usually have the audience on the floor, and the invited personalities are honored in special seats on the stage. But in Singapore, all the participants, including resource people, are on the floor facing the stage; whoever has a turn goes to the stage and presents himself on the microphone that is there ready.

Then I faced the problem of how long a time to speak. In Nepal, we spend much time in addressing. But in Singapore, I found "ladies and gentleman" is enough, and the speaker at once presents the subject matter. When it was my turn to speak, I felt uneasy because the style was quite different from my previous experience, and then I realized *that it was better to be clear by asking before I started my speech because there might be some assigned time limit for me.*

The president was sitting in the front row, and I asked him in a low voice, "Mr. President, how long can I speak?" One of the young participants sitting close to the president heard my question and got up and replied, "Mr. Guest, you can speak as long as you like, but we can't stay more than five minutes."

It is not important how long we want to speak; what is important is how much the audience wants to listen. I also came to know that the speaker may enjoy the speech, but the audience may have difficulty in listening. So we have to pay attention to the interest of the listeners.

You can compare a businessperson to a fine chef, and customers to diners. A chef is required to cook in accordance with the feelings, needs, and motivations of the diners; otherwise the meal may be in vain. Similarly, no matter what taste and interest a cook has, he or she is required to cook according to the appetite and taste of the diners.

In business, it is obvious that we need to identify our tasks, do our business as per the demand of the customers, and market. Who produces what is not important, but knowing what is in demand in the market is valuable.

Many people start a business according to their own preference, and there is one popular proverb that says "choose as per your own interest." But I think that is an old and traditional saying. Nowadays many philosophers and meditation gurus suggest, "He can be happy and successful who controls his own interest)." If we want to be successful entrepreneurs, we should start a business that sells what the market wants instead of looking to our own interest. He is a good businessman who can seek his interest in demand, instead of his own choice.

Case Study
(from http://en.wikipedia.org/wiki/Carlos_Slim)

Carlos Slim Helú *is a Mexican businessperson. He got the title of 2011's richest person in the world, with his fortune estimated at $74 billion.*

First he bought shares in a Mexican bank. In 1965, he bought Jarritos del Sur.

In 1966 he founded Inmobiliaria Car.

By 1972, he had established or acquired a further seven businesses in these categories, including one that rented construction equipment.

In 1976, he branched out by buying a 60 percent interest in a printing business.

In 1980, he branched out further into industry, construction, mining, retail, food, and tobacco.

In 1985, he bought Reynolds Aluminio, General, Bimex hotels, and Sanborns, a food retailer.

In 1986, he also bought a chemicals business, Química Fluor, and others.

Later, in 1990, he acted in concert with France Télécom *and* Southwestern Bell Corporation *in order to buy a landline telephony company.*

He changed his behavior according to consumer demand. Similarly, we should change our interests according to demand.

A human life starts in infancy, and an infant is an unknown being in terms of choice and interest. There is no choice or interest at the time of birth. But later on, he might have choices and interests that he learns through culture, education, and environment—but not by birth. As an example, a baby likes to take his mother's breast feeding. Some days later, if you start to feed him with cow's milk, he doesn't like it for a few days—but a few days later, he will get used to cow's milk. So we have the power to change our interests, and we need to have it as well.

To become distinguished entrepreneurs, we are always required to be flexible in our mission. For example, if you are interested in the hotel business in a location where there is no demand, then you need to change your mind toward either another business or a different location where there is demand.

For example, there is a popular tourist city named Pokhara, which is my birthplace. Many successful business houses and many big hotel owners were running their businesses according to their own interests and choices. Before starting business, they assumed that they would be successful because they had their own unique management skills and conducted their business differently from the way others did. But finally many of them flopped. Why? So far as the hotels were concerned, it was because of the overriding number of beds, which far exceeded the number of clients.

In the same place, several small businessmen are running businesses like spas, cottage restaurants, curio shops, and lots of other businesses that meet consumer demand. They are successful.

Everyone thinks that his business has its own uniqueness and can easily compete with others, but this is not always true. People needn't be so smart in making their business unique rather than one that consumers demand.

When people see and evaluate others' success, they normally start the same business almost in the same area. Later, when the result appears, it may be harmful to both businesses, and there may not be any remarkable progress.

People think interest cannot be transferred and it may not be a good thing. But this is not true. I want to tell you one obvious example: Many lovers join in and share the deep interests of each other and feel that they cannot live without each other. They vow a great love to be sustained forever. Finally, after a long time, that same couple may get divorced. Why does the same interest die in the same person? It means interests may have changed according to time and context. If it is true in serious matters like love that interest may change, then why not in business? Interest can be changed by willpower.

Willpower originates from desire. Willpower is required to make a leap in life. Willpower is not a thing that is genetically obtained; it actually depends on the society where the individual lives. So you can transfer your own choice into another. You can gain your willpower from your strong desire.

A businessperson has to determine his profit according to the benefit of the customers. What customers need can easily be estimated. You can imagine yourself as a customer and then determine the need. If you are a customer, you always seek something that is effective, efficient, cheap, long lasting, useful, attractive, and so on. Whatever you like, this is the same as the likes of other people. So you can improve your product according to the demand of the market by modifying its design, by facilitating it more, by making it more efficient, and by developing it to be more practical, valuable, and attractive. If you are in the process of producing something, first of all carry out research to diagnose the necessity and interest of the customers, instead of your own.

BUSINESS AND PUBLICITY

In business, there are two types of publicity—advertisement and recommendation. Advertisement is your own language, whereas recommendation is a permanent customer's language. This language is much more effective than advertisement, and is uttered as per the gratification of the customer. But attractive publicity should be done so it will be noticed. Let's see how a company does advertisement and its impact.

Case Study
(from http://en.wikipedia.org/wiki/Pepsi)

Walter Mack was president of Pepsi-Cola since 1940. He supported progressive causes and noticed the company's strategy of using advertising for a general audience.

He employed Hennan Smith, *an advertising executive from the Negro newspaper field.*

With the slogan of "Leaders in Their Fields," they started advertising profiles of twenty prominent African Americans, such as Nobel Peace Prize-*winner* Ralph Bunche *and photographer* Gordon Parks.

As a result, Pepsi's market increased dramatically as compared to Coke's. After the sales team visited Chicago, Pepsi's share in the city overtook that of Coke for the first time.

From the 1930s through the late 1950s, "Pepsi-Cola Hits The Spot" was the most commonly used slogan in the days of old radio, classic motion pictures, and later television. Its jingle was used in many different forms with different lyrics.

They utilized the services of a young, up-and-coming actress named Polly Bergen *to promote products, oftentimes lending her singing talents to the classic "Hits the Spot" jingle.*

In 2009, "Bring Home the Cup" changed to "Team Up and Bring Home the Cup," the new installment of the campaign. Pepsi has official sponsorship deals with three of the four major North American professional sports leagues: the National Football League, *the* National Hockey League, *and* Major League Baseball. *Pepsi also sponsors* Major League Soccer.

How much money do we need for advertising? As much as is needed to gain our profit.

There are genuine singers and musicians. They may have their disciples and fans all over the world. But we don't hear about such personalities. What we hear are the junkies who have sung ten or twelve songs but have made eighty-five advertisements. They sing in accordance with the demand of the audience, walk along with the changes, and in this way have been popular with a few songs. In business, each entrepreneur is required to make publicity about it. In business, people may not only advertise, but also they can compose songs about their products. Recommendation, however, is more effective than self-made songs.

A customer is free in making a choice. The producer needs to understand the choice of the buyers or purchasers. The first sign of success in enterprise relies on the analysis of customers' choices. Your own choice should follow the choice of the customers.

One of my friends started a hotel business in an area where there was no demand for hotel rooms. Thus, he was not selling the rooms and the meals. I finally heard he sold the hotel project and got a good price. Now he has money, but I don't say he is a successful entrepreneur. People may have lots of money, but that doesn't mean that they are successful. Money can be earned through different means. If we want to distinguish a successful person from a chance-hunting fellow, we need to agree that the above person should earn from the selling of the rooms instead of the project sale. I am sure if he were running the hotel, he would be unsuccessful because the product was not in demand. He sold the project instead of the product at a good price, but that is not a business—it is politics in business.

People may regard their business a means for earning money in any way. But this is not true. I think a true businessman is one who remains busy and follows the principles of business. There are people who run after money without any business principles. I think they are like crocodiles that attempt to hunt elephants on land.

We know about bees' activities. They work in groups and make honey because they follow the queen bee as a leader. A queen bee never provides training to them and she never provides any motivation to her followers, but they still work. Why? The only reason is that they are self-motivated. A business-aiming person needs self-motivation to commence the business, and there are some clues to self-motivation.

I was invited to a leadership training program in Matsoya, Japan. I was a little afraid, thinking that I might be refused the Japanese visa. We

Nepalese have this fear, and it has been our culture. I had to prepare for the presentation in Japan, had to study some additional materials regarding business leadership, and wanted to be mentally prepared.

At last I got the Japanese visa stamped on my passport by the embassy of Japan in Kathmandu. I knew the visa was only a permission to enter the Japanese airport from Kathmandu. The immigration authority at the Japanese airport might not permit me to enter Japan. They might turn me back.

Once I reached the Tokyo airport, the inspection officers at the immigration office asked me two questions: (1) Why are you visiting Japan? (2) Where is your training schedule? I spent quite some time there, answering questions and being investigated.

A bit later, I was received by my Japanese host, and the manner and behaviors they exhibited made me forget the episode at immigration. I entered Japan and looked around. This is the country of the rising sun, green hills and mole hills, covered in flowers and small houses like playthings for children. Japan was unity in diversity.

When I had an overview of Japan, it looked as if the natural Japan was all embellished with technology. I was fascinated not only by the natural Japan and its miraculous technology, but also by the manner and conduct of the Japanese, who are generally very polite, honest, and faithful. The inaugural ceremony was decorated with thousands of vases that contained flowers of different colors put together. The culture was rich and affluent.

The thing I liked most about that seminar was the concept of leadership without any restraint. There were 116 participants, each representing his or her own country, and it was a great opportunity for me to represent Nepal. The seminar emphasized freedom and democracy, and it focused on leadership without any restraint. If leadership isn't free in itself, if it is dominated, then the leadership is like a caged bird.

During our study, in our textbooks, we studied that there are four types of leadership, but in reality, there are many more types. There is not any hard and fast choice in this regard. The United States has its president as the leader of the nation. In India, it is the prime minister who works as the chief executive of the nation. Japan prospers with its old monarchy.

China is booming ahead, in spite of the one party of Communism, with its tiger economy. In Nepal, we have a number of revolutions and changes. The Communist regime in Cuba has done nothing except push the country backward, and the absolute monarchy in Bhutan has always been chasing its own people out of the country.

The following tips will be useful to consolidate and update leadership. We will explore each of them in more detail.

- Motivate yourself—"if he can do business, I can too."
- Start your business simply, and hand it over as a memory.
- Don't crow like a hen; work like a man.
- Be an ant's head rather than an elephant's tail.
- Regard yourself as a leader, not a laborer.
- Realize yourself—everything is possible, but nothing is guaranteed.

Motivate Yourself If He Can Do Business, I Can Too

God has gifted everyone with similar bodily features (except the disabled ones). Everyone is endowed with necessary bodily limbs like eyes, hands, legs, brain, heart, and so on. There is no usual and normal human being with three eyes, three ears, three hands, or two heads. As two people with two similar legs don't necessarily reach the same destination in the same time, people with similar bodily limbs don't necessarily make similar progress. There are certain factors that affect a person's abilities beyond their physical bodies.

Did Sir Isaac Newton have a different skull from ours? Did Diego Maradona have a different leg from ours? Did the Wright brothers have different hands from ours? Was Bill Gates born with a bundle of notes?

The above personalities didn't have any more superhuman limbs than we have. They invented things, maintained new records, and brought revolutions in the world. The main clues to such success are determination, courage, and the use of wisdom. We need to have the concept and feeling "If others can, why can't I?" Remember that you aren't inferior to others in any way and God hasn't discriminated against you. He has endowed you with all the things required for a human being. If we don't have adequate enthusiasm, energy, willpower, perseverance, patience, toil, and determination and if we stay idle, we may be doing injustice to ourselves since we have been endowed with all the requirements.

We can't borrow the above qualities from anyone; neither can you buy or alienate them from anyone. We may transplant our eyes, hearts, or other parts of our body, but we can't transplant these qualities. We don't survive only for the sake of survival; we must determine to do something in our lives. We can follow the paths of some great personalities; we can think from what is high and make a strong commitment in our lives. What we can say about leadership is that it needs to be bold and determined, like Abraham Lincoln of the United States, Mahatma Gandhi of India, and V. I. Lenin of Russia. Leadership is required to be change-prone.

Start Your Business Simply, and Hand It Over as a Memory

Case Study
(from http://en.wikipedia.org/wiki/Coca-cola)

The founder of the Coca-Cola Company, **Asa Griggs Candler**, *was born in* Villa Rica, Georgia. *His business career was as a* drugstore owner. *In 1887, he bought the formula for Coca-Cola from its discoverer,* John Pemberton, *and other shareholders for $2,300. The success of Coca-Cola was basically due to Candler's aggressive* marketing of the product. *Candler made millions of dollars from his investment, allowing him to establish the Central Bank and Trust Company, invest in real estate, and become a major philanthropist for the* Methodist Church.

A leader needs to understand that wherever he is stepping, he should enter as a general member; by the time of departure, he needs to be a memory for having contributed to the organization with remarkable deeds. If a leader performs effectively, with very remarkable performances, he or she will be able to leave the organization a memory, which may extend as far as abroad. Originality and efficiency are two key elements toward the success of our performance. To remain in the memory of the stakeholders and others shall be a great success in life.

Don't Crow Like a Hen; Work Like a Man

There are people who go on talking for hours. They cluck like a hen without laying any eggs. If you concentrate more on talk, it is obvious that you have low concentration on your work. We always hear the saying—"talk less and work more."

As we know, this is a world of communication. Talks, speeches, and interviews are quite common and one of the basic requirements; when we are talking with others, we are communicating. We are sharing our ideas and feelings, maintaining social relationships, and promoting friendship between the interlocutors.

But there are certain things we need to pay attention to before we talk. Mind what you are going to talk about, who your interlocutor is, why you want to talk, how much time you should talk, and what may be the output. We always need to have a useful and purposeful talk. Just a blubber or cackle may not be useful. Sometimes if we talk quite carelessly without any purpose and preparation, our own words may outweigh our dignity, and they may put us in problems. Words once uttered from the mouth can't be taken back. Thus, we need to think twice before we speak, and we need to observe what effect our words will have. When we talk or give speech, we need to deliver only what is possible and practical, and then our words are required to resemble our deeds. We need deed-resembling words, goal-attaining words, and brief but effective words.

Be an Ant's Head Rather than an Elephant's Tail

A human being is a rational creature. Your own brain is enough for your development. You need to go ahead as per your own decisions and rarely depend on others. Your freedom is more important than others' suggestions and guidance. You are a leader, and leadership is required to be located on the lead ahead. No matter how small your team or group is, you need to be the head of the group. An ant's head is all right, rather than an elephant's tail. If you depend on others, you will always be a tail. The literal meaning of leadership also focuses on this fact. Leadership needs to function with its own conscience, wisdom, and decisions. Being an owner of a small company is far better than being a jobholder in a big industry.

Regard Yourself as a Leader, Not a Laborer

Mind refresher:*"Immoral business leaders are always in motion without emotion."*

A leader doesn't work himself, but arranges work for others. There are activists, workers, and laborers who work as assigned by the leader. The contractor or foreman is a leader in a construction company where a number of workers work. A man isn't ideal in everything. A leader can't work well, and a worker can't lead well. A leader may have a broader scope of working, whereas a worker works within a more-restricted periphery. A leader's role is to lead, supervise, direct, and implement. Therefore, a leader has an implementation role, whereas a worker plays a complementary role.

Realize Yourself Everything Is Possible, But Nothing Is Guaranteed

I was giving a lecture on "this is a world of logic" in Cambodia once. I was arguing that whoever presents convincing logic wins the debate. When logic is weakened or impaired, loudness governs. Logic is reasoning things, and by using this device, we can justify our motion and convince others to consent with us. Almost every thing or event can be reasoned. If not reasoned well, even truth may be falsified.

Once I was in a training session, and I was presenting my subject matter. I proposed a motion that water is far more harmful than wine. "Do you agree?" I asked. The participants were speechless for a while and then uttered, "No." I knew they didn't agree with me. Then I started reasoning: If a man drinks *wine every day, he may die after twenty or twenty-five years due to his drink, but look at the floods and cyclones like tsunamis, Katrina, and so on in the world. Isn't it water that is killing thousands of people at once? Does wine kill so many people in one event? Wine may take somebody's life, but slowly and gradually over a number of years; but water-caused floods and cyclones are killing thousands of people together at one time. There are also many people who are suffering from waterborne diseases. Now what do you think? Isn't water more harmful than wine?*

In the past, our forefathers believed that the earth was flat and the sun was going around the earth. Galileo presented his logic and said it was the earth that was going around the sun. It was very odd logic at the beginning for the people to believe, but later they believed. We read in our books that there were nine planets in the universe, but there came the news that scientists are saying they have discovered another planet. Now we believe this new thing. What makes people trust is logic.

In our society, there are people who are quite courageous and very determined. They want to do something in their life. They have their own ambitions and aspirations. But I don't see all of them being successful in their mission. Only a few of them may be working out the true meaning of their desired destination. Almost everyone may have their own dreams and vision about their career. But the remarkable thing is that such dreams and vision need to be practical and applicable in life; otherwise, they will turn into fantasy and will never be fulfilled. Living an optimistic life with the hope of reaching your destination is far better than living a pessimistic life.

> ***Chaudhary Group*** *is one of the renowned and successful business houses of Nepal. It has played a vital role in products at an international level. Once it produced a brand of beer named Singha. It is a famous beer of Thailand, like Tuborg and San Miguel of Nepal. Chaudhary Group didn't succeed in selling its product in profusion. This product especially proved a fiasco. For*

any product or company to be a success, there needs to be a combination of several elements: quality, abundant investment, capital, management, market, marketing strategy, and so on. Didn't the Chaudhary Group have such elements?

Of course, they had good management skills. But why did they fail? In my experience, a person making efforts with several elements is not enough for success. This effort carries only a 50-percent role; the other 50 percent may depend on luck. If I believe in luck rather than my effort, people may blame me for being a conservative person. But I don't care, because I have lots of good experiences in this regard as I have had conversations with successful personalities. I have found that they believe in luck to a certain extent. I have a strong belief that every success is the result 50 percent of effort and 50 percent of luck—and a man may not be lucky or unlucky forever. Chaudhary Group lacked luck in that product, and this is the reason Singha beer was an unsuccessful product.

Entrepreneurs need to believe in luck as well. Speaking truly, 50 percent of business depends on luck. Sometimes it may be that customers may buy and hoard your product. Suppose your sale is cold drinks and your business is going slowly. Suddenly there is a terrible drought throughout the country. More and more people get thirsty and drink your bottles, which are eventually sold in abundance. You may call the incident luck. The drought that you never imagined proved to be lucky for you.

Many young people are afraid to start businesses. The only reason is that they are afraid of being unsuccessful. I have some questions for them:

- What is your reason for being scared?
- Why don't you start the business?
- If you fail once, is it the end?

CASE STUDY
(from http://en.wikipedia.org/wiki/.James_Wilson)

James Wilson is founder of Standard Chartered Bank. He was from a wealthy family background. His brothers established a manufacturing factory, which they dissolved in 1831. Wilson continued in the same line of business and reached a pinnacle of success. During the economic crisis of 1837, he lost most of his wealth when the price of indigo fell. By 1839, he sold most of his property and avoided bankruptcy. He became a normal person. However, in 1853, he founded The *Chartered Bank of India, Australia and China, which later merged with* Standard Bank *to form* Standard Chartered Bank. *He again became highly reputed and a successful businessperson.*

Youth is a period that is like a football team playing a game. In the football game, as we see it, one team hits and makes the goal, and then it is the turn of the other team to score a goal. Whoever scores more goals within an assigned period of time is the winner. Similarly, in your youth, you cannot measure your success. There is not such a measurement tape that has ever been invented by scientists. Sometimes you may succeed and sometimes you may not. Your success cannot be finalized until you have declared your retirement. It may be at the age of sixty-five or thereafter that you may do hands-up, and only thereafter that your business game is over.

People believe "everything is possible" in the world. But it is also true that "nothing is guaranteed." A businessman should have the feeling of this statement before commencing a business. Then he can have a motivation to go ahead. If he fails, he can realize the next step.

CHAPTER THREE

Who Can Become a Businessperson?

One day Gautam Buddha was in meditation under a tree. One of his disciples came to him and asked, "Are you a God?"

Buddha said, "I am not a God; I am a human like you."

The disciple again inquired, "So are you a great human being?" Buddha replied, "I am not that either. I am a human being like you."

The disciple wasn't satisfied and again asked, "And then are you so famous because you were born in a palace?" Gautam Buddha smiled and said, "I have forsaken the luxury of the palace, and I am just a human being like you."

Each time Buddha said, "I am a human being like you." The disciple was surprised at the replay of Gautam Buddha and finally asked, "Then who are you in reality?"

Buddha replied gently, "Believe that I am a human like you. The only difference is that you have a concern in the word 'you,' whereas I am concerned about who I am. I am searching into myself. I am inquiring of myself on matters like why I was born, what I should do, and so on, and I am trying to identify myself. I have discovered that life is not only for survival; we need to do something in our life. I have been walking about searching for peace and *happiness and their foundations. In this way, as I am in my own pursuit, I happen to be a guru, and as you always regard about others, you happen to be a disciple."*

If anyone plans to do incredible things in his life, he is required to identify himself, as Gautam Buddha has remarked. A person needs to identify:

- Who I am,
- Why I was born,
- What I have been doing,
- What my responsibilities are,
- What objects are,
- What moral norms and standards I have to follow,
- and so on.

In business as well, a person is required to identify the above concerns about himself. Running a business without knowing oneself is like walking along a street with blind eyes. If you do so, you are quite unlikely to reach your destination because you haven't known the path and you haven't known yourself.

A business planner or entrepreneur needs to identify himself—who he or she is, how capable he or she is, how much can be invested, how much coverage can be performed in the business, and so on.

God has endowed each creature with his own feature. The dog sleeps awake, the kingfisher is brilliant at catching fish, the crow is clever, and so on. God is the nature that has maintained a balance in the world. He has created things from microorganisms to giant creatures.

Once a rich man had a swimming pool in his park. His eight-year-old son almost accidentally drowned while swimming. But the child was saved by a gardener who was nearby. The father was so grateful that he offered the gardener whatever he liked, especially money.

The gardener said, "I'd rather not accept money from you. If you want to help me, I have a son like yours, but I can't pay for his education. If you have some interest in this regard, help me send my son to school." The rich man consented and thus helped the gardener send his son to school.

Time went on. The son of the rich man was now twenty-eight years old, an adult. He became sick and was about to die. Doctors tried, but his disease couldn't be cured because medicines of that kind weren't available. He was near death.

Meantime, a new medicine was produced and put on the market. The sick youth was provided with the medicine, and finally he was safe. He avoided the death.

The inventor of the medicine? The son of the gardener who had been admitted to school with the help of the rich man.

This is an example of "education as wealth and obligatory for all." Human beings are different from animals to this extent.

Everyone has a goal. He wants to successfully reach his goal, but he gets puzzled—he doesn't know from where to commence and where the destination is. He may not know the right path to reach the destination. This puzzle is caused by his own inability to identify himself. The most important clue to your success in reaching your destination is to identify yourself first and then have self-motivation and enough commitment to achieve your success. You need to have strong willpower to turn your aspiration into achievement.

You can observe the creatures in the world around you. An animal may have one special feature as mentioned above because it has been gifted with that ability only by nature. But you are a human being. You have been gifted with a number of skills and abilities. So you need to distinguish yourself from animals.

We're all born with some natural capacities. Yet some men lag behind others in the course of their progress. Your progress is the outcome of your toil, brain, inquisition, and dedication. The mere human body can do nothing. You are required to activate your body organs in accordance with their appointed works. The Wright brothers weren't born with airplanes, Newton wasn't born with a measuring tape to measure the level of gravitational power of the earth, and Bill Gates wasn't born with money. The success they gained was only the outcome of their brains, hard work, and devotion.

A fish is gifted with the ability of swimming. So the moment a fish comes out of its egg, it starts swimming. You can watch a fish swimming. You get fascinated by the way it swims. You become jealous of it because you also want to swim. You happen to make a boat, a yacht, and then a big ship that floats on the sea and travels thousands of miles. This is the miracle of mind, body limbs, and the heart of a human.

Nature has made birds to fly. To But as humans attempted flight, they made airplanes that could fly farther and higher than birds and are flying even today. This is the brain of human beings, which has made huge planes that have outsoared eagles in the sky. Therefore, what is required is commitment and determination to turn your knowledge into expected outputs. We are used to making alibis from time to time, but we actually need to utilize the talent we are endowed with.

People Who Have No Money

http://en.wikipedia.org/wiki/Dhirubhai_Ambani), *born in1932, was the son of a very low income and simple village teacher. He really wanted to study for a bachelor's degree, but his ambition melted when he looked into the anxious eyes of his sick father. "I'll do as you say," he said. Due to the financial crisis in his own home and requests by his parents to make money, he left the college life in opposition to his interest.*

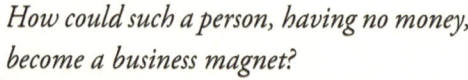

How could such a person, having no money, become a business magnet?

One day, Ambani's mother asked him to help his father by earning money, and he angrily replied, "Why do you keep screaming for money? I will make heaps of money one day." On weekends, he began setting up onion and potato fries stalls at village fairs and made extra money, which he gave his mother.

Then he became one of the outstanding entrepreneurs who founded Reliance Industries, a petrochemicals,

> *communications, power, and textiles conglomerate and the only privately owned Indian company. Today the company, with over 85,000 employees, provides almost 5percent of the central government's total tax revenue in India . His life has often been referred to as a true "rags to riches" story.*

Is money required to become a businessman?

Many entrepreneurs get discouraged at the beginning due to the lack of money for investment. "I haven't got sufficient money for investment, so how can I start a business?" Of course, sufficient capital is required to invest in a business, but there are lots of entrepreneurs who are operating their businesses using other people's money. When a businessperson initiates a business, he or she is not required to invest the entire money from his or her purse only. You can have 10 lakh rupees with you, and there are banks that will offer you 40 or 50 lakhs of rupees and you can operate your business with their money. You have to pay the bank their interest, but you can make your earnings on other people's money. Therefore, to start a business, money is not the prerequisite. "Entrepreneurship" is the most important thing to run a business. "Use others' money" is the principle for an optimistic entrepreneur.

The main object of a business firm is to earn profit and get financially strong. A school is founded with the object of maintaining quality education, but if it maintains quality in sports and ignores the education part, it is not a school anymore. Likewise, if a bank is involved in social works rather than in financial activities, it is also outside of its object. Similarly, if a business firm doesn't aim at earning profit, it isn't a business firm anymore.

Mind refresher: *If you just advance me a loan of five hundred dollars, it will get me completely out of debt.*

If you are interested in starting a business, as stated above, it isn't required that you have enough money of your own. Suppose you have Rs. 15,00,000.

For the rest, you can either accept a loan from a bank or a relative or you can install your firm with commodities on credit. You only need to analyze the potentiality of your business; you are likely to prosper then. There are fewer people who are operating businesses out of credits and loans. Some people are afraid of the idea of investing on a loan, but an entrepreneur needs to be daring and he or she should face the encumbering risk in business. A genuine businessman never has cash money; when he has money, without delay, he invests in business and he can manage for the rest whenever required. This is the capability of an admirable entrepreneur.

A road is never made by itself and naturally. It is usually constructed when someone has to travel to his or her destination. Or in other words, it is constructed as per the necessity of people. There are many ways out to operate a business firm:

- Taking a loan
- Taking on a partnership and cooperative
- Taking on an active partner

CASE STUDY

Min Bahadur Gurung *is the owner of Bhat Bhetani, the largest and most popular department store of Nepal. A normal man from the countryside twenty-five years ago, he borrowed a loan of USD 500 and started business. He used the loan according to his calculations and has become the largest store within twenty-five years and is the highest taxpayer in the department store sector.*

TAKING A LOAN

A responsible person always prefers to utilize a loan rather than his own funds. Where there is awareness, there is an enormous possibility of success. That may inspire the person to be more active in his business. In other words, a gentleman agrees with promises to return the money if it is a loan. A loan is like a simal tree, tall but vulnerable in structure. If we care for it and feed it, it grows well. If not, that big tree may fall down upon your house and destroy you.

You can earn infinite profit from a loan by paying only fixed interest and installments to your bank. Some people may analyze that this kind of loan is good, and some people may have a misconception in this regard. This depends on human nature, but a capitalist's nature should be different from that of a normal human being. The following tips may be useful in this regard:

1. Reason/purpose of borrowing a loan: Should be for investment in business, not expenses in the personal field.

2. Creativity: Consider whether you are a creative person destined for success or not.

3. Properties: You need to have enough property to be on the safe side.

4. Ability: Your business needs to have enough capacity to return a profit.

5. Assets: Your loan should be of smaller size than your capital.

If each moment of our life is risky, why don't we take risks to set up a business? The amount of risk may be a concern. Do you calculate your risk or hope for luck regarding your risk?

> *When **Dhirubhai Ambani** returned from abroad to India, he started Majin in partnership with Champaklal Damani, his second cousin. In 1965, Champaklal Damani and Dhirubhai Ambani ended their partnership because they had different temperaments and a different take on how to conduct business. While Mr. Damani was a cautious trader and did not believe in building yarn inventories, Dhirubhai was a known risk taker; he believed in building*

> *inventories, anticipating a price rise, and making profits. Now we don't remember who Mr. Damani was.*

Almost every successful person in the world is a risk taker. A risk taker may fail ten times, but he can make up for it all in one success; a person always concerned about safety has a tortoise nature.

In a simple calculation, if the above points are true for you, you are on the right path to take a loan. The main motive for taking a loan is that "a certain sum of money is likely to attract more money," and business is the only field for that purpose. If there is no business, there is no use taking the loan.

Nowadays, lots of banks and loan providers have plenty of good schemes. They may be offering up to a 100-percent loan if they find the project is feasible. If we want to be excellent entrepreneurs, we need not be anxious thinking about matters like "I don't have money." Taking a loan is the best way to manage money for a daring capitalist who has no money.

Taking on a Partnership and Cooperative

> *A farmer, having a meager income, normally cannot dream to be a businessman alone. The same thing happened in part of India Gujarat before 1946. Many of the same occupation planned together and joined in a cooperative to open a dairy business, which became one of the largest chocolate companies, Amul, in the world, with a turnover of USD 1.2 billion per year.*

Another method to develop capital for a business venture is in collaboration with others, a cooperative. If you are very committed to regulation, then you have to concentrate on cooperation. No matter how much a single man's brain weighs, it is less than the weight of two men's brains. In the same way, the analysis of many men always calculates things better than a single man. If you don't have enough money and are searching for investors, a partnership project is best for you to manage money. If you want to be a businessman and you just have 1,000,000 rupees but the project cost is 10,000,000, find nine friends like you for a cooperative.

Here are some tips to assist in finding coop partners:

- All partners never have the same attitude, but rules should always be the same to all.
- Don't try to govern by yourself; try to find the best governor.
- Always manage by full leadership quality, but not by quantity for a short time.

These are real facts to convert your friends into partners; otherwise, a friend will be converted into an enemy, and in that way, a cooperative never lasts for the long term. Rochdale Pioneers, an early consumer cooperative, listed seven principles of a successful coop venture:

1. *Voluntary membership*
2. *Democratic member control*
3. *Members' economic participation*
4. *Autonomous and independent*
5. *Education, training, and information*
6. *Cooperation among the cooperative*
7. *Common in community*

Taking on an Active Partner

Another way to generate capital for your business is taking on a partner. There is an extreme difference between a hungry boar and a well-fed one. Naturally humans want to live without any trouble, but the man who is hungry doesn't care about trouble in the way as he is always in search of food. There is a mass of capitalists who have lots of money. They want to invest money in good projects. A younger man who is more energetic and has a feasible project can propose the wealthy people just invest and he will run the project by himself on a mutual-agreement basis. This is the best way for a man who has no money to become a businessman.

People Who Have No Time

People say that time is alterable or changeable, but I say it is always going round the same. There are days and nights and again the same thing. There are summers and winters coming and going. Time moves like a beacon light. There are twenty-four hours in a day, and for some people, that's a very long duration; whereas for others, it isn't adequate and they may wish that there were forty-eight hours in a day. In Bill Gates's software, there are five thousand hours in a day. In today's world, it is time that has become a significantly important element.

Einstein defined "Time is the fourth dimension of an object."

- It cannot be bought or sold.

- It cannot be saved up or stored.

- It cannot increase.

- It cannot be stopped.

Time is limited for a person, but businesses are infinite. You can't accomplish all your works within a limited time frame. An entrepreneur has at least the following jobs: production, protection, and profiting through sales. These are his main jobs, and they consist of a number of other subordinate jobs. One brain, two eyes, two hands, and two legs may not be sufficient for the numerous jobs. But a brain with ideas and a heart with courage and enthusiasm can handle a number of tasks. Generally speaking, we may say that one person can do one job, but in practice, we are seeing that one person is handling a number of jobs or big companies at the same time. This is leadership in business, which can within a limited amount of time manage a number of workers to operate the business.

Mind refresher:
Do you drink tea?
Yes, seventy cups a day.
Why don't you drink a hundred?
Because I don't have any free time.

An entrepreneur doesn't require a lot of time himself to run his company; he can do his job within a limited amount of time with the help of others. The main technique in business is the efficiency of employing and leading others. Leadership in business doesn't have to work twenty-four hours itself; it can work ten hours a day but get the job accomplished with the help of employees. Therefore I would like to say, *"The man who is busy still has time to share, but the man who is needlessly busy has no time."*

I've found that these are the major factors in wasting time:

- Emergency meetings
- Parties and picnics
- Not making decisions
- Impossible courage
- Meaningless work
- Unnecessary loans
- Excessive time talking to friends
- Long talking on the telephone
- Gossiping
- TV serials

Managing Time

Michael Althsuler said that "The bad news is time flies. The good news is you're the pilot."

Many people make a list of jobs at night for the following day's duty. If we make the list of our forthcoming duties at bedtime, naturally the list plays and replays in our mind the whole night. That may create problems in sleeping. I suggest people make a list of the day's program on the basis of the following tips in the early morning. Follow the full day's plan accordingly, and reschedule incomplete works for the next day's priority.

- There are too many duties, but I can manage them all.
- There is no more time; I am going to start now.
- This is a little assignment, but it is ample and very precious.
- *Highest priority to do immediately*
- Listen and apply comments
- Incidental emergency
- Order of your boss
- Order of your clients
- Projects nearing completion
- *Start work with sense*
- Design a plan of action
- Prepare a plan
- Do research
- Make policy and strategies
- *Please, refuse*
- Hasty work
- Bluff news against you
- Valueless invitations
- Programs with no results
- Jobs with no deadline
- *Don't*
- Work without laborer
- Gossip or use cigarettes or alcohol at work
- Undertake unnecessary education

People Who Never Work

Standard Chartered Bank has 1700 offices and more than 70,000 workers worldwide. The chairman, Mervyn Davies, does not know all the workers and the branch locations, but he gets profit through all his workers' duties.

Leadership in business requires having the art of employing others. A universal truth is that a man is not perfect doing everything. You may not be skilled in your business yourself. If you are skilled in leading others, you may get things done that you actually don't know how to do. You don't know how to teach, but you can set up and run a school. You don't know how to cook, but you may lead a hotel restaurant. You don't know how to drive, but you can own and employ a number of buses and bus drivers. This is leadership in business.

Mind refresher: *A new lady secretary said, "The boss says I am a little behind; I don't know if he meant I should work more or eat more."*

On the other hand, staff are required to work sincerely and faithfully. The leadership or the employer needs to satisfy the workers with adequate payment and motivation. A person with the traits of leading a business, planning ahead, motivating the employees, and meeting the object of earning money and expanding the business is an entrepreneur. Do you know the owner of the Coca-Cola company? Do you know the founder of the Toyota company? How about the founders of other similar big companies? You don't know them! But don't worry, even the owners of those big companies also don't know who their workers are and where the branches are located. A leader never needs to work himself, but he has capacity about team building and teamwork.

How a team builds

Nature of member

- If all have common targets and goals
- If all concur on roles and responsibilities
- If all task, communication, and decision systems work
- If all have the desire to learn skills

Nature of leader

- If arranges profiles according to qualifications
- If applies equal rules to all
- If honors the majority and loves the minority

How a team works

- If they have a winning desire from the core of their hearts
- If they get lots of theoretical and practical knowledge, training, and instruction
- If everyone feels he or she is the major player

CHAPTER FOUR

CAREER PLAN IN BUSINESS

Do you want to win a game, or do you want to win life?
First person: "I want to win a game.". Wrong!
Second person: "I want to win life." Good!
Third person: "I want to win life by a game." Best!

As we know, human beings have four stages of life, that is, childhood, youth, maturity, and seniorhood. Yes! Nobody can repeat a stage. Whoever wins the challenges of each stage wins the life. The challenges at each stage are different.

- In childhood: happiness, learning a positive attitude
- In youth: study, enjoying sexual activities
- In maturity: marriage, family, economic
- In seniorhood: -social activities, advising

Some research shows that there are many people who started businesses in the earlier period of the youth and achieved great success in the economy. But business is a tedious job. It carries lots of mental tension, which constantly affects the other activities of the maturity stage. We don't have to disturb our honeymoons, we don't have to lose our young friends, we don't have to lose the physical needs of each stage. If we win all these, then we can win the life too. *Life is more precious than a game. The art of living means winning both games and life.*

Sometimes we are favored by our fortune or luck, and sometimes we are victimized by our misfortune. The total sum of fortune and misfortune is our fate or destiny. Believing in fate or destiny is one thing, but it is inextricably attached with our life. A traffic jam was my destiny. A destiny is a kind of coincidence that usually comes out of expectation. No matter how aware and careful you are, there may be problems, and it is due to your destiny. If you win a lottery, it is your fortune.

Our life is entirely associated with both of these things—deed and destiny. *A businessperson, I think, should believe more in deed than in destiny.* Deed determines your day-to-day, life whereas destiny interferes in it.

Differences in Manners Between a Normal Man and a Businessman

Character varies from person to person. There are as many characters and manners in the world as there are people. Whatever profession people have, their ultimate pursuit is happiness and bliss. One person's satisfaction may be an impediment for another person. The fulfillment of needs are the immediate satisfactions. When someone is hungry, the attainment of food is the immediate satisfaction. A person under the pressure of urination will be happy at the attainment of a toilet.

Generally there are two types of attitudes found in people:

Businessman	Normal man
Ready to face the challenge	Unable to face the challenge
I should do something	I will do something
Able to confess defeat	Not willing to get defeated
Ready to fight problems	Afraid of problems
Discontent, always mongering	Content
Studious, experienced, and systematic	Wait and see
Work prone	Pretending

Figure 1. Types of attitudes

The manner or attitude of people is affected and shaped by external factors, such as the culture, tradition, friendship, education, family, society, and other things. A person with one kind of manner will be subject to circumstances and thus may happen to bring change in his manner. The first manner or habit may be inhibited in a person in one way or the other, and it gets exhibited on occasions. Such inhibited manners have important roles in promoting a business. The manner and interest of a person need to get accommodated with his business. A person needs to be free in making his or her choice. *Sometimes I reply to a forceful person, "My freedom is more important than your good idea."*

In developed countries, experts make a study of the children's psychology before sending them to school. They want to find out the interests of child— what he wants to do himself—and then he will be provided education as per his own interests. One child may have his interest in study, another wants to be a musician, another may be fond of doing business, and so on. Similarly, since there a number of businesses, a particular person may have his interest in a particular business. Entrepreneurs are to be allowed an opportunity to run businesses as per their own will and interest.

There are some people who have interest in putting themselves at risk. But there is a difference between risks chosen randomly and risks chosen deliberately. The risks undertaken after analysis may result in benefit, whereas the other risks may lead you to uncertain destinations and most probably to loss. The analysis depends on planning ahead, whereas random choice of risks is like gambling. A successful entrepreneur is the one who plans ahead and analyzes about the potentiality of the business. Suppose you have a total capital amount of fifty lakh rupees and you invest all your capital in business. If the business goes into loss, you are bankrupt.

Willpower, enthusiasm, and inspiration are important personal traits required in business. A nervous and discouraged person can't venture to face risks. Lack of education, experience, an insecure future, pessimism, inferiority feelings, and so on cause the venture ahead. It is better for a person with less confidence to start his career with a job and build up experience, confidence, and enthusiasm. *Enthusiasm and laziness are two parts in a person's life.* If a person gets successful in his mission and achieves things as per his expectation, there is enthusiasm and optimism. On the contrary if the things are not gained as per one's expectation, the person is engulfed by nervousness and frustration.

Our attitude determine our utterances, such as I'll do it later, I am not in the mood, and so on. These are the expression of antiqueness. They indicate exhaustion. The same person is sometimes more enthusiastic and works much harder. The same person, on another task, may turn out to be very lazy and goes on staring. Enthusiasm and laziness both are human qualities, and they are caused by particular circumstances.

If we crave to do something right now, it is our willpower that is getting very active. Generally a person needs to start his business when he is mentally ready and has strong willpower. A willful beginning of business may lead us to an eventual success. If we go on collecting our willpower and do not start anything, it is like hoarding the dirt that eventually stinks.

An entrepreneur can't collect his jobs. He works like a swimmer who moves against the current ahead. A businessperson ventures ahead, removing and solving all the problems that are on the way. He needs to solve *all* the problems—both those created by self and those caused by others. Normally you do not create problems yourself. You are usually troubled by problems created by others.

Business is operated depending on its customers. We are judged by our customers; we can't judge ourselves. In reality, our business is like a spider's web, and our success depends on how many butterflies we trap into it. Our business may face a number of problems, such as problems of insufficient or unqualified workers, the shortage of commodities, the inadequacy of capital, problems regarding the environment, policy and rules, technology, competition, and so on. We need to struggle against these problems and overcome them; we needn't escape them, because then we aren't daring and successful entrepreneurs. We may be attacked by problems again and again, but the most important thing is that we need to face them and work against them or solve them. The solution of problems may bring relaxation and comfort to us. We may learn a lot of things from the problems. Our struggle against the problems will eventually make us experienced and veteran businesspeople.

Let's see how big companies face these problems.

*From 1999 to 2002, **Samsung** conspired with Hynix Semiconductor, Infineon Technologies, Elpida Memory (Hitachi and NEC), and Micron Technology to fix the prices of DRAM chips sold to American computer makers. In 2005, Samsung agreed to plead guilty and to pay a $300-million fine, the second-largest criminal antitrust fine in US history.*

In May 2010, the EU antitrust watchdog levied a €145.73-million fine against Samsung for the same DRAM cartel.

In December 2010, the European Commission fined six LCD panel producers, including Samsung, a total of €648.925 million for operating a cartel. Samsung received a full reduction of the potential fine for being the first firm to cooperate with the EU antitrust authorities. (from http://en.wikipedia.org/wiki/Samsung_Electronics)

A soldier performs a physical fight, whereas a businessperson competes with his brain. A mindful person with the qualities of determination, perseverance, and enthusiasm, amalgamated with business motive, is an entrepreneur.

Some people may be operating their business as diurnal daily phenomenon. A person has a shop, and he stays in the shop all day long, spending time on trivial transactions. He has been running the shop for more than twenty-five years but hasn't made any remarkable progress nor has he extended his business. It can be seen as a daily existence rather than a business.

Only making profit and running a business are not sufficient to prove we are businesspeople. Our business needs to be extended as per the income we make. Some people are not satisfied with any amount of income. Other people will ask them, "How much wealth do you need? You still seem to be dissatisfied." In reality, this is the quality of an entrepreneur who is industrious and dutiful. The person with further expectations and desires for success can be the right person for business.

Study, research, and experience are other determinant elements in business. A businessperson needs to study and research about the business he is going to operate. There are people who may underestimate and think that an elephant doesn't study—Bill Gates prospered without any university degree, so why do we need education? But study, knowledge, and experience regarding the business are a must, and we can prosper if we have these things.

We may learn a lot from our own experience that may help to prepare for the next step. We need to be aware of another factor learn from other people's experience. It is not necessary to experience everything yourself. For a healthy business career, it's better for you to learn from your own experience, and then you can benefit by learning from the experience of other people.

SIX FLOORS IN THE BUSINESS PYRAMID OF

> *I met a maternal uncle of mine in the United States. He was a man of fifty and had been in the United States for more than eighteen years. His family is well-to-do people. While in America, I asked him to return to Nepal, as he was fifty years old and had been away from home for so long. He replied, "My dear nephew, you don't know that fifty years of age in Nepal is twenty-five years in America. There is still a lot I have to do and go through."*

Then I came to know how important enthusiasm and the spirit of doing something are. Age does not matter; my maternal uncle is still very active in his fifties. Though my uncle is a master of enthusiasm, physically age matters. A twenty-five-year-young man can't be compared with a fifty-two-year-old man. An eighteen-year-old youngster does not have similar expectations compared with an eighty-one-year-old man, and a sixteen-year–old teenager's expectations are certainly different from those of a sixty-one-year-old mature man. A person is required to perform in accordance with his age and career planning.

How long a person will survive is always unknown. A person can't be active forever. In childhood and old age, he or she is less active, weaker, and exhausted. He is underpowered. His physique and brain aren't mature enough or are all fatigued. The brain does not favor you as age wears on; both physique and brain get weakened and you can't work as much as you used to. In other terms, *when the physique is more active and sound, you can do manual jobs or physical performances; when your physique gets fatigued, you can activate your brain and play advisory roles. This is known as the career plan.*

Based on my experience, one's career plan can be as follows:

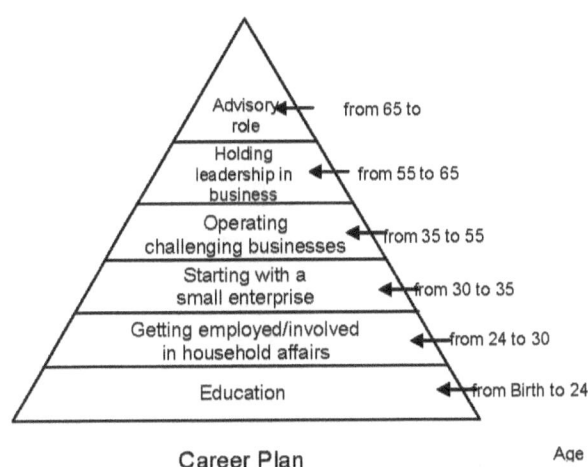

Career Plan   Age

FROM BIRTH TO TWENTY-FOUR YEARS OF AGE

Generally people attain their education in seventeen or eighteen years of time. Children at the age of five and six start going to school and study until they are twenty-two or twenty-three years old. The superlearning concept of education has divided mental development into two stages: below fourteen years of age and above fourteen years. Until the age of fourteen, the human brain is very active and fresh. It is like new hardware that can store any data very easily. A young person until the age of fourteen or fifteen can learn things very quickly because learning ability is remarkably high. Information and data can be picked up very easily.

The older the person grows, the frequency in the functioning brain gets slower and slower. Aged people can't catch things as fast as young people can. They are used to asking questions again and again. Until the age of fourteen or fifteen as per the concept of super learning, youngsters have very high-scale memory, but in the later ages, memory power almost fades out and the power of analysis becomes dominant. Elders, therefore, have more logical statements than the younger ones.

The memory earned from youth gets amalgamated with the experience gained in different stages of life, and later it enables logical thinking. Education does not mean getting degrees and certificates; it is the means of obtaining knowledge. Many businesspeople say that Bill Gates got his success without education, but he is very sincerely involved in deep education.

> ***Bill Gates*** *was born October 28, 1955 Seattle, Washington. He is chairman of Microsoft, chairman of Corbis, and cochair of the Bill and Melinda Gates Foundation,*
>
> *He is also a director of Berkshire Hathaway and was CEO of Cascade Investment. He has a net worth of US$56 billion. In a May 2006 interview, Gates commented that he wished that he were not the richest man in the world because he disliked the attention it brought.*
>
> *He studied at Harvard University but later dropped out. Gates graduated from Lakeside*

School in 1973. He scored 1590 out of 1600 on the SAT at Harvard University.

There are many legless people who teach others to run. Teaching others to do something may be an easy job, but adopting the same thing in one's life may be a painstaking job. A doctor asks his patient not to smoke, but when he gets a chance, he smokes himself and can't control it. The reality behind it is the doctor is an educated person who himself happens to smoke.

The fresh brain or mind until the age of fourteen or fifteen, as described above, is not free in itself in our society. Our social structure, families, and education methods aren't favorable to keep our brains free and fresh. There are unnecessary pressures for learning things, threats, shouts, punishments, fortunes, and so on, all of which may spoil the young brain, handicap it, and finally paralyze it.

In reality, the young brain needs to be free from all kinds of pressures and tortures. Youngsters aren't to be assigned heavy jobs. Youngsters are to be allowed free times to think, to experience, to learn of their own choice, and even to analyze what is right and what is wrong. They should be taught about humanities, the art of living, love care, beauty, hygiene, society, culture, morals, and so on. They need to have opportunities for free learning. Then they will be able to maintain their lives themselves, learn in free and liberated environments, and eventually prove a milestone in creating a healthy and peaceful society.

In some developed countries, I have seen that there are youngsters of fifteen or sixteen doing the job of hawkers and restaurant workers. That may not be a compulsion except in a few cases. Most of them do jobs in their early ages for experience.

Theoretical knowledge is quite different from matters of fact. In my college days, as far as I remember, my teacher was teaching us how to make water by mixing oxygen and hydrogen. When we were in theory class, the matter was as clear as daylight; but when we went to the lab, it was quite difficult for us to make water from oxygen and hydrogen. We couldn't mix them properly in proportion for quite a long time. We succeeded, but only after great endeavor.

There may be differences between theoretical study and practical execution. Theoretical study should resemble and coordinate with the practical aspect. If theory and practice are in adverse mode, there may be some unexpected accidents. In the lab, if there is any mistake during the process of making water, the same hydrogen is likely to generate a bomb, which may explode in the end and destroy everything around. What is to be emphasized is that only theoretical knowledge or formal schooling isn't enough in life. The most important thing is how we apply our learning and knowledge in our practical life.

Age from twenty-four to thirty years

After the completion of study, one is required to plan for a career. Experience is essential for this purpose. You can work for your relatives or get employed by yourself to accumulate experience. Many people want to start their business without experience, immediately after completing their study. They don't want jobs because they feel bad in others' work, but many great business personalities started their carriers through jobs.

Warren Edward Buffett *is an American business investor, financier, and generous donor. He is widely regarded as one of the most successful investors in the world. He is the primary shareholder, chairman, and CEO of Berkshire Hathaway. He is consistently ranked among the world's wealthiest people. He was ranked as the world's wealthiest person in 2008 and was the third-wealthiest person in the world as of 2011. He started his business carrier employed from 1951 to 1954 at Buffett-Falk & Co., Omaha, as an investment salesman; from 1954 to 1956 at Graham-Newman Corp., New York, as a securities analyst; from 1956 to 1969 at Buffett Partnership, Ltd., Omaha, as a general partner; and from 1970 to the present at Berkshire*

Leadership in Business

Hathaway Inc, Omaha, as its Chairman and CEO. (fromhttp://en.wikipedia.org/wiki/Warren_Buffett)

Your experience will enable you to go into the depth of reality. But getting involved in a relative's business or getting employed by someone may not always be an easy thing.

Employment is a problem in many countries. Nepal is not an exception in this regard. A great number of people are unemployed in Nepal. If there are any vacancies, there may be thousands of applicants for a few posts. But the tendency of seeking jobs in Nepal is quite traditional. Most people have interest in government and permanent jobs even though the remuneration is less attractive. If there are vacancy announcements on behalf of a private company, there are usually far fewer applicants.

I have had experience at my own company in this regard. Once I made a vacancy announcement, and there were only a few applicants; another time, there was not even one applicant. I think it is due to the traditional mentality of the people who seek white-collar jobs, easy desk jobs, and outwardly prestigious-looking jobs. People may dream of having jobs in higher posts and designations, but it is quite difficult for them to get their dreams fulfilled.

There are job vacancies, notices, and many want ads in newspapers every day. Moreover, this is the time of the Internet and cyberlinking, where one can browse jobs on websites. Some people say that you need to have a lift from your own people to get employed. Nepotism and favoritism may work in many cases, but your qualification, ability, and experience outweigh such aspects associated with employment. If favoritism and nepotism were really practiced, there wouldn't be advertisements all over the newspapers. Sometimes blaming nepotism and favoritism may just be a way out, an escape from being disqualified in a job competition.

A friend of mine, Mr. Hari Kafle, is older than I. So far as I know, he was in a project and then he was in a bank. Later he got employed in the US embassy, and eventually he got a chance to work in the United Nations. I know very well that he was never favored while applying for jobs. Wherever he competed, he was selected in the first position.

You have freedom to work wherever you like. It is better for you to continue the job you are doing until you have better opportunities. It serves you with experience. You can quit the former job when you have another better job by informing your previous employer. You have energy, willpower, and enthusiasm for work. Since it is the age of toil and hard work, you shouldn't indulge in enjoyment and relaxation all the time.

AGE FROM THIRTY TO THIRTY-FIVE YEARS

Blashack Strahan *started her gourmet food company with $6,000 in savings, a backyard shed for storage, and a pool table as a packing station. In her own words: "I remember sitting outside one day, thinking we were three months behind on our house payment, I had two employees I couldn't pay, and I ought to get a real job. But then I thought, No, this is your dream. Recommit and get to work."*

She had the idea to sell at taste-testing parties, and sales began slowly picking up. In twelve years, Tastefully Simple has grown into a $120 million dollar business. (from http://www.rd.com/money/secrets-of-successful-entrepreneurs/)

This is the best age period for opening a business, so we are frequently starting and operating a small business during this time. We have a small investment, and there aren't many workers required. If we employ a number of workers, we may go into loss. We need to work hard ourselves, though we may undergo a lot of hardship. We entertain it, as it is human nature; sometimes we may smile in pain. Smiling in pain is kind of a hobby. A mountaineer also smiles and enjoys the painstaking uphill climb of a mountain. This is a trait of a daring and gallant person.

We accumulate our experience of operating a business firm and enterprise. Or we may be operating a factory. We are learning by doing, and then doing by learning too. There may be much risk of loss in business, but we face all these challenges. We do not get exhausted. Ang Rita Sherpa climbed Everest more than eleven times but didn't get tired and wanted to climb more. A number of people from all over the world are arriving and attempting to climb Everest. There is much risk in climbing Everest; it may take your life. But people are climbing it, ignoring the consequences to fulfill their destiny.

There will be no achievement without facing the risk. You are starting a business and thus are going to face risks. Your business will be extending so far as your health and brain cooperate with you. Initially you apply your physical labor to a great extent in your business to get it established, but later, as you have it extended and you have a number of employees, you are going to employ much mental labor and exercise. When you are leading a firm, you need the characteristics of leadership. You need to supervise the transaction, production sales, and purchases along with the performance of the employees. You need to determine your production and business policies, make decisions, and apply new and practical as well as sustainable marketing techniques. You are on your way to leading a business house.

This age is regarded to be a mature period for marriage too. If already married and he or she has begotten children by the age of thirty, he or she is required to be mature, with new responsibilities. She or he has multiple responsibilities toward the husband or wife, father and mother, and children. One's spouse may be the first and most important partner at this stage to start a business, which can be maintained with one's own family members.

Having a reliable and trustworthy partner in a business is a different thing. We can't trust anyone outright as your partner. Our family members may complement us in this regard. Let's see an example of a spouse becoming a good partner.

> *High school sweethearts from Petaluma, California, Mena and Ben Trott, got into blogging after losing their jobs at a small San Francisco-based web design firm in the dot-com bust. Husband-and-wife team Mena and Ben Trott developed Movable*

> Type as a tool for Mena's personal blog posts. When they offered it online, there were over two hundred downloads within the first hour. From their apartment, the Trotts launched software company SixApart, now a multinational provider of blogging tools, with more than 10 million estimated users. (from http://www.businesspundit.com/12-amazing-success-stories-of-unlikely- 14)

AGE FROM THIRTY-FIVE TO FIFTY-FIVE YEARS

The age between thirty-five and fifty-five is the age of maturity. This is the age in which we have a business, job, transactions, and social dealings with people. We are growing more and more mature now.

> **Bill Gates,** in age between thirty-five and fifty-five, was number one on the Forbes 400 list from 1993 through 2007 and number one on the Forbes list of the world's richest people from 1995 to 2007 and 2009. In 1999, Gates's wealth briefly surpassed $101 billion, causing the media to call him a "centibillionaire."
>
> **Ambani,** in the age between thirty-five and fifty-five, in 1975 was visited by a technical team from the World Bank at the Reliance Textiles's manufacturing unit. This unit has the rare distinction of being certified as "excellent even by developed country standards" during that period.
>
> **Carlos Slim Helú,** in his age between thirty-five and fifty-five, was running nine companies and having excellent success.

From the above case studies, we can assume that this age is the most vital period in business. At this time you already having experience in jobs and small business, and by nature you are physically and mentally perfect. As you mature, you will start challenging the business with your expert strength. This is the highest earning period in life. So we need to do challenging businesses in this period.

A challenging business means:

- Investment in large size
- Having branches
- Having many employees
- Large transactions

For instance, we can talk about the prerequisites required for the candidate for the US presidency. A candidate needs to fulfill only three criteria for the presidency: he or she must have been born in the United States, be over forty-five years of age, and not have been the president twice before. The age barrier of forty-five years indicates that the candidate should be mature enough and well-experienced enough to be positioned at the post of president. Maturity is required to carry out any business in a successful way.

Age from Fifty-Five to Sixty-Five Years

Our physical strength, mentality, and enthusiasm will all deteriorate in the course of time. A person can work very actively until the age of fifty-five, and thereafter, he or she will get fatigued both physically and mentally. There will be a great burden of the family and children, and due to the prevailing circumstances, a person can't work as hard as usual at this age. You are not fit for manual work anymore. You can't operate the physical works yourself, and you may be better at desk jobs and leadership. This is the time of leading your business firm doing less physical tasks and more mental tasks. Things aren't stable and static. They are usually revolving, just as the earth itself revolves. The circumstances are therefore changing, and you need to adjust yourself in accordance with the circumstances.

Age from sixty-five to above

The age gap is a major factor that keeps distance between the aged and the youth. People naturally like others to adjust with them and perform the tasks in the manner they expect. Old people complain that youth are superficial, impatient, and hasty; whereas the youth may regard the aged as outdated and stubborn. The youth are always attempting to modernize things, whereas the aged are always sharing their experiences. It is better that the adults get involved in active jobs, whereas the youth need to modernize society in a digestible way.

CHAPTER FIVE

TURN YOUR BEHAVIOR INTO BUSINESS BEHAVIOR

"God provides food to every bird, but he doesn't throw it into the nest; those birds can find the food that go to search." —Shiv Khera

Similarly God offers equal opportunity to all people to prosper and thrive in their lives. The only difference is that only a few people identify such opportunities and thrive, whereas many of them are lost like birds in clouds.

I have a friend named **Madhu**. *He went to Japan in 1991 and came back only in 2002. When we met each other after eleven years, I found that there were changes in his physique. He had grown fatter and whiter. The cold climate of Japan made him whiter, and the balanced composition of meals, excluding fat and carbohydrate, also helped him appear energetic. His appearance, physique, and gestures are all different today.*

I noticed that he was always fidgeting with his hands while talking or sitting idle. His fingers were always in motion. I was surprised and asked why he couldn't

> *restrain his palms. Then he looked at me, as if he wasn't asked this question by anyone before, and replied with a sigh, "You see, I worked in Japan as an egg peeler for ten hours a day. It was my job. In these ten years, my hands have known nothing other than peeling eggs. My fingers are used to this work, and they are very willing to peel the eggs that I can't have at present. Now it's obvious that if we do the same jobs for a long time, physically and mentally, we are used to it.*

Human behavior is not determined by birth; it is generated from culture, practice, environments, and so on. Similarly business behavior comes from relation with businesspeople and business environments. Changing behavior from one to another might be possible through willpower. Let's see how a person can effect positive change in his behavior.

> *There was another friend of mine. He was used to smoking. He attempted to give up smoking several times, but he couldn't. We all used to call him a chain-smoker. Wherever he was, he had cigarettes in his mouth. Many of us advised him to give up smoking. One day he initiated it himself by browsing a website on ways of giving up smoking. He got the ways of how to reject a smoke website and made a list of them as follows:*
>
> *1. First, make a determination and commitment.*
> *2. Recall it from time to time.*
> *3. Drink a lot of water.*
> *4. Take sweets and bubble gum.*

> 5. Forsake smoking friends.
> 6. Instead, spend time talking with nonsmoking friends.
>
> *He applied the above solutions, though it was quite difficult to put them into practice, he said. After a few days, he was able to give up smoking. It was possible because he was self-motivated and initiated it himself. What is important is self-motivation or self-initiation.*

When there are positive aspects in change or revolution, we need to adopt or follow them. In other words, we are required to catch the positive turns in change and modification. An intellectual person adopts changes only through observation and a general public adopts changes only after they themselves are affected, but a fool always denies changes.

In my opinion, there are four behaviors in a human being:

- Parallel   I am right, and you are also right.
- Proud   I am right, and you are wrong.
- Nervous   I am defective, and you are effective.
- Worse   I am wrong, and you are also wrong.

What thought or habit is right is determined by circumstances in most instances, but a general businessperson is required to follow and adopt the generally accepted behavior of an enterprise.

The same person may perform good and evil acts, depending on the circumstances and his mood. The following factors are decisive in generating evil acts in a businessperson:

- Selfish view
- Vain pride
- Feeling of revenge
- Association with addicts

The above traits cause negative behavior of a business leader. The following behaviors will have to be adopted by successful entrepreneurs:

1. Take over if you are perfect; hand over if you are not perfect.

2. Invest others' money.

3. Invest; do not spend.

4. Aim to be an entrepreneur, not a millionaire.

5. Don't push sales; allow customers to buy.

6. Follow the traditional traits of entrepreneurship (smiling, dedication, time management, and sacrifice).

7. Never be nervous; be spiritual.

Take Over If You Are Perfect; Hand Over If You Are Not Perfect

A man may not be perfect forever. Many businesspeople having some bad behavior don't want to lose their post even though the company is running at a loss. Most successful company leaders love their company rather than their post; it is one of the most essential behaviors of a business leader. Let's see an example of that kind.

Kiichiro Toyoda *was a Japanese entrepreneur and the founder of Toyota company. Each year, this company produces 7,308,039 units (2011) and turns over US$235.89 billion. It has total assets of US$370.3 billion. The year 1950 was one of flagging sales and loss of profitability, . He resigned from the company. His cousin and confidant, Eiji Toyoda, became head of Toyota Motor Corporation, overseeing its successful expansion worldwide and the*

launch of Japan's most prominent luxury vehicle brand. When he left the post, a new, energetic executive came and fulfilled the success.

Invest Others' Money

Standard Chartered Bank in Nepal has total paid-up capital of just Rs 1.6 billon, but they collect a total of Rs 40 billon from depositors and invest depositor money for bank activity. They pay some of the interest to depositors but receive a net profit of Rs 1.1 billon from their investments.

A business house took a 70-percent loan from the same bank as part of their equity; that company paid a fixed rate of interest on the loan and regular repayments, but got a lot of profit through using the bank's money.

If you have a certain amount of money, you may invest it in a business. You haven't borrowed anything from others. Now you have no risk because you aren't in an indebted status. You work quite comfortably. You rarely hurry up, and you have no worries either. But you are unlikely to gain success. The old proverb says, "No pain, no gain." In your business, your loans are your pains. Pains will lead you to gains, and eventually you will make a success of your business.

Risk is the source of hard work and industry. Hard work leads you toward profit and success. If you have 10 lakh rupees and you start your business by investing 20 lakh rupees, you will have double benefits: you will establish a well-equipped company and you are likely to make more profit as it awakens you all the time. Borrowed money never lets you stay idle. Most entrepreneurs therefore run their business with loans from banks or other lenders. The basic tenet of business is to invest others' money; apply this strategy and earn from others. Expenditure never returns, whereas investment returns along with some additional profits. A business firm or company requires investment especially at the foundation period, and thereafter it may start giving you a return.

Invest; Do Not Spend

Nokia, a leading mobile company, has annual revenue of €42.45 billion and markets worldwide. They are using a phone software of Android.

Microsoft, the other biggest American company making communication software, paid about a cool $1 billion to Nokia to not *choose Android.*

An expenditure and an investment are similar in that both go out from you. Expenses never return, but investments may return with additional benefits. Sometimes business looks like gambling, but it is a game with low risk and high return calculations. From the above Microsoft example, we may learn that a businessperson always has investment behavior as demanded by the situation.

Aim to Be an Entrepreneur, Not a Millionaire

Suppose you wish to earn a million dollars. Then your sweat will stop when you have done so. But if you aim to be an entrepreneur, your efforts will be forever expended toward making wealth. A successful businessperson should aim to be an entrepreneur, rather than aiming for a limited dollar target.

Is there any limit of wealth? There is no limit of wealth as long as there is no limit of satisfaction. You can ask a person, "Are you satisfied with your money?" The reply will be, "No." Ask another person, "Are you living a content life?" And the reply will be, "No, I have some problems." Exactly! We know that no one is absolutely content in his life. Bill Gates in the United States is always aiming further. The sultan of Brunei has been expanding his business, and so are the Ambani brothers in India. No one in the world is financially satisfied until he or she forsakes the world or worldly needs. The important thing is that life is not for money, but money is for life. It is not everything in the world, but everything has financial value today.

Don't Push Sales; Allow Customers to Buy

A businessperson is required to honor the freedom of customers. They want to enjoy their right of choice at the time of purchase. You needn't force them to buy anything. A forced sale will anger the customers, and they may not come to you the following day.

> *Once in our neighborhood, there was a popular shop. It was a kind of department store, where almost everything was available. The shop was popular for its quality products and reliable sales. There was a crowd of customers every day. The proprietor of the shop in the past was said to be a quality vendor/seller, and the legacy had been maintained to date. The shopkeeper today is not a famous one himself. He is selling in the fame and name of his parents. I haven't seen his parents, but the very names are popular in the locality.*
>
> *Whoever goes into his shop purchases a lot of things; and if you touch or point out anything there, the shopkeeper insists you need to buy it. There is not any doubt about quality and the price is cheaper than anywhere else, but the customers have stopped going there nowadays. The shop is still selling quality goods at a cheaper price, but customers prefer to go elsewhere because they aren't allowed to enjoy their right of choice due to the crowd of customers and the traditional behavior of the owner.*

Follow the Traditional Traits of Entrepreneurship (Smiling, Dedication, Time Management, and Sacrifice)

A business may sustain itself for a long time if the entrepreneur understands the mentality and needs of the customers and the latter are able to identify the quality goods and the reasonable price. A chili is hot, a lemon is sour, sugar is sweet. Heat, sourness, and sweetness are the qualities of the above things. If something is not hot, it is not a chili anymore; if it is not sour, it isn't a lemon anymore; if it is not sweet, it is not sugar either.

If a person does not display business qualities, he or she can't be a businessperson. Even a gentle smile will help you grow your business.

Always smile at your customers because it:

- gratifies others and you lose nothing.
- may help in communication in later days.
- may stay in the memory of the customers.
- is the remedy to people problems.
- doesn't cost money but is very valuable.

Flowers are beautiful but can't smile, nature is fascinating but cannot speak, and mountains are magnificent but cannot move. Only humans can smile, speak, and move. A businessman doesn't need to put a vessel of flowers at the gate nor welcome the customers with a banner. Smiling a welcome is a priceless element, and it is the best gift for your paying guests.

If you smile or laugh with pretension, your customers will understand it. Don't laugh a fake laughter. Smile naturally and cordially, and it will be a great source in growing your business. A natural and usual smile emerges from a gratified and content heart. Leonardo was gratified by the smile of Mona Lisa, Shakespeare wrote a number of sonnets in the name of his beloved (the black lady), and the Taj Mahal was built for posthumous gratification. In this way, contentment generates smiles, and smiles affect the outer world.

Never Be Nervous; Be Spiritual

People get frightened and nervous when they face problems. A nervous mind usually gets terrified, and it has an eventual consequence on the whole body. A nervous or terrified person can't solve any problem but may worsen it. However, at least being nervous/terrified/hurried is a signal toward readiness for a solution to the problems.

Shame and fear are different matters and are signs of nervousness. People say the nose of people bears shame. Thus, there is a saying "What a noseless/shameless person!" But I think the eyes, not the nose, contain shame. If anyone is ashamed, it is expressed through the eyes, not through the nose. Most human feelings are expressed through the eyes.

You can look at a cat and its eyes. You can have eye-to-eye contact with the cat. You go on looking at its eyes, and after a while, you express your fear and say, "Yeah!"

People have fear. They are afraid of others. It's a feeling that is connected with power and might. The weak are always frightened, whereas the mighty ones dominate others. A lion is not afraid of anything in the forest, whereas a deer or a rabbit is afraid of almost everything. The weaker are always scared. If you have a weaker mentality, you get afraid or frightened. The world is dangerous for those who are afraid of it. Don't feel weaker, because the world is precarious for those who are scared of it.

So far as change or revolution are concerned, change starts from your own feelings or emotions. You need to win over your own emotions or convert the idle emotions into revolutionary ones. It's a tough job to do so. It's difficult to protest against your own feelings. So how can you protest the feelings of other people? You can't win over your feelings and emotions if you don't have a strong commitment and the knowledge of spiritualism.

Science has taken over all the world. Science has brought miraculous changes. It has made the life of the people prosperous. But does prosperity bring happiness? Different people may have different occupations and conduct. But the ultimate pursuit in life of most people is peace and prosperity. Science may have gifted people with prosperity, but it has failed in maintaining peace in the world. Only spiritualism may bring happiness and peace to the suffocated life of people in the world.

An old proverb says "knowledge is power," but it is not true. Knowledge is just right information. Willpower is power, and willpower is generated in the human mind by the practice of spiritualism.

Suppose we say to a person, "Smoke is injurious to health, and you should not be a smoker." If this kind of knowledge had power, that man should be able to stop smoking, but that is not what we see at all. Only a few people forsake something through knowledge; what they need is willpower.

Businessmen need to have lots of willpower to control their behavior, so it is essential to be spiritual. A businessman can turn spiritual by:

- Trusting in God
- Studying religious books
- Being pious
- Light worshiping
- Practicing meditation
- Eating tamasik food

The above business behaviors are the path of success and playing a vital role in leadership. Business is a kind of dependent and interdependent process with the customer; without the customer, we even cannot assume to operate a business. A businessperson should know the behavior of his or her customer as well as his or her own.

Consumer Behavior

"Consumer behavior is the process whereby individuals decide whether, what, where, when, how, and from whom to purchase goods and services." —C. Glen Walter and Gordon W Paul

People purchase goods for themselves or their family as needed. The reaction under the goods is the behavior of the customer. These are the clues to find out customer behavior:

Why do they want to buy?
    As needed
    Comparative quality

    Cheap price
What do they want to buy?
    Goods that are in demand
    Fashionable goods
Where do they want to buy?
    Easy access
When do they want to buy?
    Seasonal
How do they want to buy?
    Facilities
From whom do they want to buy?
    A shop with goodwill.

CHAPTER SIX

THE DESTINATION OF BUSINESS

Three important concepts regarding the destination of business are:

- Business is an open space with an infinite destination.
- Anyone can open a business, but the extension through earned profit is the only destination.
- Don't put all seeds in the same jar.

How much do you want to earn in your life? Is there any limit? What is your aspiration or ambition in life? What do you want most? A homeless person may wish to have a house, another person may wish to have a car, and a few of you may wish to be a great industrial owner. One of my comedian friends told me, "You know how to become rich? I'll tell you a joke."

Mr. Ramesh has really become rich!
Why do you say that?
Because he keeps a servant for his bicycle.

You may found or set up a business, run or operate it, and earn a profit or go into loss; well-wishers may suggest improvements to you, and some nearer and dearer may assist you in promoting your business—but so far as the determination of goal or destination is concerned, it is up to you to choose.

Birds can fly in the sky—it is a natural gift to them rather than their interest or choice—but a human can't fly in the business sky even if he has made a dream and wished for wings as his interest. We can accept some ideas, suggestions, and help from others. But where our destination is and how far we can go, we have to make a path by drawing a map ourselves. Not all shining things are diamonds. No matter how colorful the confetti is, it is never like real flowers. You may have an aspiration to earn money and you may earn it too and have all the physical facilities, yet you are not a good industrial person unless you have aimed to be one.

A human has two eyes. When he drives a car, there are four eyes, including the two headlights of the car. The looking glass is another eye to look back; and in this way, there are five eyes altogether. In this way, five eyes are required to drive a car, and many more eyes may be needed to operate an industry or business. There should be eyes everywhere to run a business firm, and thus the risk shall be mitigated.

When John F. Kennedy was the president of the United States, his sole aspiration was to send an American to the moon. During his presidency, he forecasted that an American would land on the moon within ten years. Neil Armstrong fulfilled his dream within nine years and nine months.

A businessman has to make a plan, create a favorable environment, and assemble resources. There are others who execute the plan, vision, and aspirations. *The plane in the sky doesn't have to construct its own way; it just has to reach its destination by flying. Similarly entrepreneurs can determine their goals in business, and there are hundreds of paths like the sky road of airplanes ahead.*

The Earning Cycle

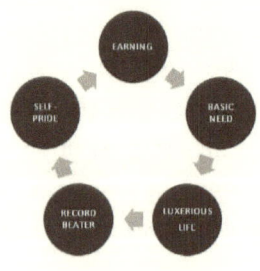

Figure-3

Leadership in Business

All efforts have causes. There should be a cause and a purpose for earning money too. There are many rich people, but they still dart for more money. Why? Just like a man's life cycle, the earning cycle also revolves, so whether a person is wealthy or homeless, he has an enormous inbred urge to grab earnings.

Sometimes we hear about the world economic crisis. If currency is revolving only within the earth and may not exist on other planets, how does it become a financial problem all over the world at the same time? Almost all people run after propaganda in spite of the facts, and they want to save their money in cash; there is no buying, which negatively affects turnover in business firms, and this is the only reason for economic crisis. Economic crisis is drama rather than fact. The major negative role is played by the media.

Case Study

Lehman Brothers Company *was a global* financial services *company founded in 1850 in the United States. It was the fourth largest* investment bank *in the United States, with a continuous succeed record for 158 years(1850–2008). When an economic crisis happened in 2008, on Saturday, September 13, 2008,* Timothy F. Geithner, *the president of the* Federal Reserve Bank of New York, *called a meeting on the future of Lehman Brothers, which included the possibility of an emergency insolvency of its assets. Lehman reported that it had been in talks with* Bank of America *and* Barclays *for the company's possible sale. However, both Barclays and Bank of America ultimately declined to purchase the entire company. On September 15, 2008, the firm filed for* Chapter 11 bankruptcy protection *following the mass departure of most of its clients, drastic losses in its stock, and devaluation of its assets by credit-rating agencies. The* filing *marked the largest bankruptcy in US history and is thought to have played a major role in the unfolding of the* late-2000s global financial crisis. (from http://en.wikipedia.org/wiki/Lehman_Brothers)

First stage: Basic needs

All human beings' existence depends on basic needs. Whether rich or a vagabond, both have food, lodging, and clothing needs. A creature cannot live without these requirements, so the first aim of humans is to fulfill this need. That's why the first step in the earning life cycle is to obtain these needs. Basically, low-earning people constantly run for this need. If a person cannot fulfill these needs, his life cycle might end or he may start some bad manners like robbery, violence, or other activities to fulfill them.

Second stage: Luxurious life

When a person has fulfilled the first stage and achieved lots of things, he develops his ambition for a luxurious life. A luxurious life is very costly, so he needs to run for supplementary earnings. A luxurious life may not be desirable all the time. A human is born not only for perfunctory jobs, but also he may have a wish for living an extravagant life as well. When he has his wishes fulfilled on one side, he may generate desires from other sides. Thus, this second stage of the earning life cycle.

Third stage: Record beater

If a person has enough success on both stages or has plenty of basic needs fulfilled and lives a luxurious life, he may still strive ahead in order to break the records. If a hundred-meter race is successfully accomplished, the runner now competes to beat the world record. Business is also a kind of game, so its player also wants to beat records and gets engaged in this kind of competition. In this stage, a businessman aspires to be an outstanding businessperson of the town, the best taxpayer, or the richest person of the country. So he marches ahead to earn capital forever seeking to satisfy his longing for more wealth.

Fourth stage: Self-pride

At this time the person has enough wealth, and there is no worry for the three earlier stages. Now he has aspirations for self-pride, which can be gained either by donating to society or distributing his wealth for his next generation. Warren Edward Buffett, one of the richest men in the world and CEO of Berkshire Hathaway, said:

> *"I don't have a problem with guilt about money. The way I see it is that my money represents an enormous number of claim checks on society. It's like I have these little pieces of paper that I can turn into consumption. If I wanted to, I could hire 10,000 people to do nothing but paint my picture every day for the rest of my life. And the GDP would go up. But the utility of the product would be zilch, and I would be keeping those 10,000 people from doing AIDS research, or teaching, or nursing. I don't do that though. I don't use very many of those claim checks. There's nothing material I want very much. And I'm going to give virtually all of those claim checks to charity when my wife and I die." (from http://en.wikipedia.org/wiki/Warren_Buffett)*

If a person has the aim to distribute his property to others, there is never enough wealth. Self-pride is the concluding stage of any kind of victory, but it is never-ending. That's why even these people try to earn more, and thus the earning cycle continues to revolve.

CHAPTER SEVEN

LEADERSHIP IN BUSINESS

Mutuality in heart, honesty in brain, and responsibility on the shoulder will lead a person to success, and they will affect even the nation because completion of assigned tasks is the key element of economic development.

Sometimes while people are in queue to accomplish some job, the first person may point to the second, the second to the third, and eventually the last one may point to the first one. But the job remains undone. There is a saying "If the job remains undone, it is always upon you; if bread remains uneaten, it is always for others."

Once I went to Sweden to meet Gulther of the Study Circle. I assured Gulther I would see him on the thirteenth or fourteenth, though we were planning to return home on that very day.

I took Gulther to be a man of fifty-five or sixty, but in reality, he was seventy years old. Yet he was active, enthusiastic, live, and animated. He asked me about our sleeping time at home. I said we go to bed at about ten o'clock and get up at six o'clock. He said he goes to bed at ten o'clock but gets up at two thirty because he views life as short and he has much more to do. He was not only old, but a victim of cancer as well. He might be thinking that he wouldn't live much longer, so he wanted to do something while he was still alive.

I have come to know that people with responsibility value their time. Every single minute is precious for them. But many people have a lot of time ahead and less work to do. The saying goes, "Little time has big value, and big time has little value." The same thing happens to us. The Hindu holy book *Gita* (Bhagwat Gita) explained that:

In our childhood, we are so much overwhelmed that we think we can change the whole world.
In our youth, we aspire that we can change our country.
In our matured age, we thought we can change our society,
but
when we are in bed waiting to take the last breath, we repent much and say that we had to change ourselves.

But by that time, everything has gone, and there is nothing to change except a live body into a defunct one. *We constantly need to identify time to act, and then we need to act in time.*

Mind refresher: *When I was young, I used to think that money was the most important thing in life. Now that I am old, I know it is.*

Leaders of business can be compared with a queen bee. The bees' whole project depends upon the queen's situation. A project of the bees can be complete as per the mutual working between the queen and the bees. A queen bee never needs to motivate, inspire, force, or punish the other bees. But human workers need lots of this motivation. Why?

Bees regard themselves as belonging to one family, and they are self-motivated. If a business leader wants to lead his organization well, he should make a family relationship with the other stakeholders, workers, and customers and motivate them with the forthcoming profit. Then, everybody can be self-motivated. If self-motivation occurs, the business will move going ahead.

Human development is linked with the attainment of prosperity. In the past, people used to work hard physically to have prosperity, but today more and more mental exercise is required to attain the sought prosperity. An enterprise is operated with the motive of gaining a return from the investment. A business or enterprise can be complete only if the triangular relationship between investor, customers, and the workers in the enterprise is as a family. They are a family of business, and there needs to be harmonious relations among them.

The Business Family

Once upon a time, there was a boat in the middle of the lake with four people in it. There became a hole in the boat that made it leak and water came inside. The two people in the front were hard at work bailing out the water, but the two people sitting in the back of the same boat were relaxing. One of them said, "Oh ... there is no leak in our part." They didn't care because they didn't realize that if the boat sank, they would sink too.

The Investor

Generally speaking, the term "investor" may refer to one who invests cash money in a business. But broadly speaking, the term "investor" may also refer to one who generates a concept, has an idea, strategy, technique of marketing, and so on. Plain investment of cash money is more or less like a bet in a gamble. In a business, the concept, idea, technique, strategy, and so on are more important than the cash investment.

An investor, prior to the cash investment in business, is required to carry out research regarding the feasibility of the trade. He may have to diagnose the demand in the market, the interest of the customers, possible obstructions on the way, the solution, and many other things before the foundation of the firm. Let's see how an investor generates a concept.

***Marlbo** is the largest selling brand of cigarettes in the world. It is made by Philip Morris, USA. It is famous for its billboard advertisements and magazine ads of the Marlboro Man.*

Philip Morris launched the Marlboro brand in 1924 as a woman's cigarette, based on the slogan "Mild As May." In the 1920s, advertising for the cigarette was primarily based around how ladylike the cigarette was. To this end, the filter had a printed red band around it to hide lipstick stains, calling it "Beauty Tips to Keep the Paper from Your Lips." After scientists published a major study linking smoking to lung cancer in the 1950s, Philip Morris repositioned Marlboro as a men's cigarette in order to fit a market niche of men who were concerned about lung cancer. At the time, filtered cigarettes were considered safer than unfiltered cigarettes, but had been until that time only marketed to women. Men at the time indicated that while they would consider switching to a filtered cigarette, they were concerned about being seen smoking a cigarette marketed to women.

The repositioning of Marlboro as a men's cigarette was handled by Chicago advertiser Leo Burnett. The proposed campaign was to present a lineup of manly figures: sea captains, weightlifters, war correspondents, construction workers, and so on. The cowboy was to have been the first in this series. While Philip Morris was concerned about the campaign, they eventually greenlighted it.

Within a year, Marlboro's market share rose from less than one percent to the fourth best-selling brand. This convinced Philip Morris to drop the lineup of manly figures and stick

> with the cowboy. http://en.wikipedia.org/
> wiki/Marlboro_(cigarette)

An investor has to take many things under his or her consideration. Along with the established business firm, he has to think of his partner, the workers in the factory or the firm, and other concerned parties. The investor is not required to work like a laborer, but he needs to lead the firm, being involved in the management level and human resource department. He can perform the job in a comfortable way, but he needn't live a luxurious life leaving everything to others. One should work for oneself. The concept "others will work and I will earn money" is not a practical thing. The investor is required to perform as a high-level worker himself.

An investor is not only a manager; he is a planner, a designer, and an administrator too. He should have knowledge of managing the firm and administering the workers. He needs to know how to lead the firm ahead even at a time of loss and difficulty. This is situational leadership.

Situational Leadership

Generally speaking, there are four kinds of leadership (democratic, autocratic, charismatic, and free rein), and democratic leadership is regarded as the most significant one. In a democracy, everyone can speak, and each one is heard. The leadership policy is determined by representing the feelings and ideas of all the participants. But there are some demerits of democracy too.

- Two foolish are powerful than one gentleman because they have two votes.
- Freedoms alter in freak-out because everybody doesn't know the proper use of freedom.
- Inter-depended goes on Depended because everyone having sharing their responsibilities.
- Easy access turn in to complicated because there is too many discussion.
- Easy to escaping from Responsible because they can blame to others.

One demerit of democracy is that the decision-making process is a time-killing factor because many people have many ideas and including everyone's idea by compromising them is like an uphill job; the dissidents are granted the right of protest at the point where they disagree. Democracy enables people with different views to formulate many small supporting groups. This may eventually cause division within unity.

If any leadership attempts to function with absolute democracy, it may not be able to move ahead. People are also required to exhibit democratic conduct. Leaders are required to adopt the system of leadership as per the situation and circumstances. The government can modify and change its policy in accordance with the situation. If the subjects are easy, peaceful, and cooperative, the government can be democratic and flexible to the people; but when the subjects are rude, stern, disruptive, and even destructive, tyrannical in nature, the government is needed to change the behaviors of the subjects.

The following table shows the stages of the company and the corresponding behavior of the stakeholders and the role of the leadership.

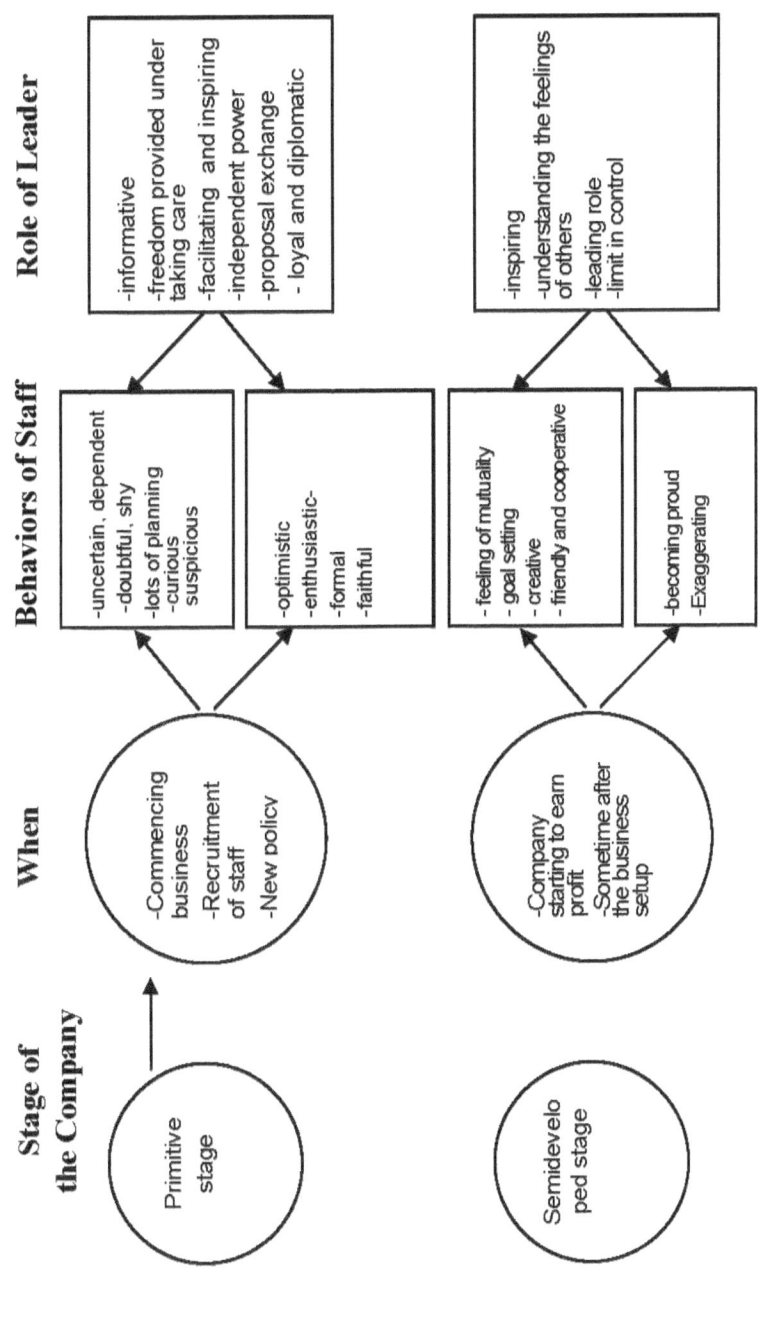

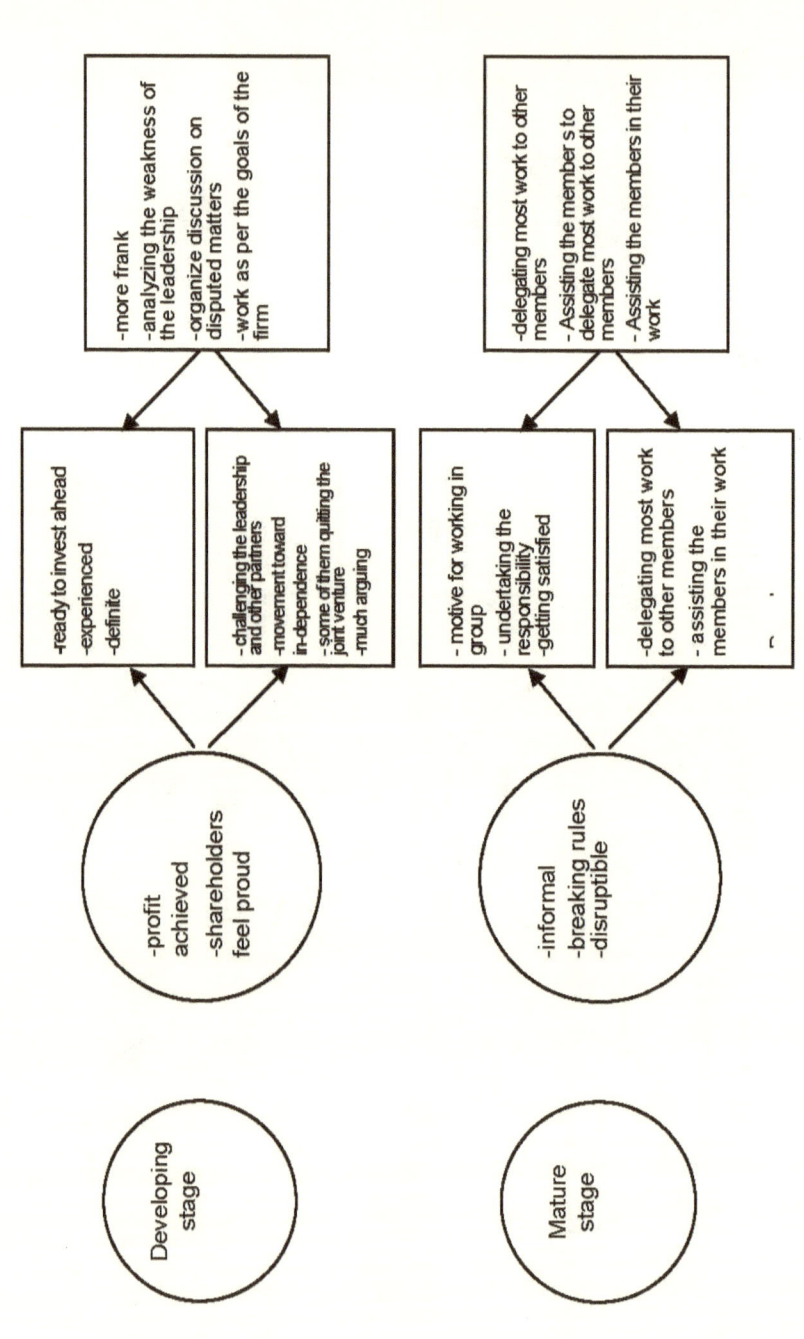

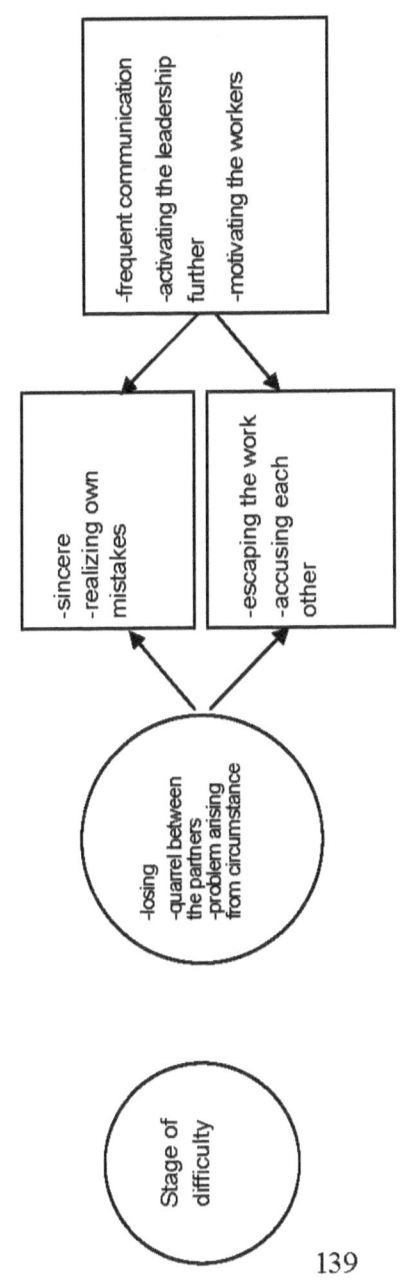

WORKERS

Ray Kroc, *founder of MacDonald cooperation, frequently reproached idle employees by saying, "If you have time to lean, you have time to clean."*

A worker is a person who works on a decided negotiated wage. A human being has two concerns in life—enjoyment/luxury and greed. But the reality is that you need to forsake luxury to attain your goal and forsake greed to attain luxury. These are congenitally received qualities as a human being. They can't be destroyed because in pursuit of luxury/comfort, being consumed by greed, development proceeds ahead. Our primary concern is not to eliminate them but to limit and control them. We need to manage our greed and comfort in coordination with the outer reality. In Freud's words, our id is to be controlled by our ego or superego.

Everyone knows that being an employer is better than being an employee. But not all people are employers. There are few employers and many employees. An employee has his own reasons for working:

- Because he is unable to run a business of his own
- Because he wants to have an experience
- Because he has to satisfy his financial needs
- Because he is not a bold person

It is obvious that many people get employed as long as there is no option/opportunity ahead. They may continue their jobs until they don't have another opportunity. Employees tend to forsake/quit their jobs when they have better chances. This is the general nature of all employees.

Employees are chance seekers. Your factory or company may be a laboratory for employees who get trained and then quit the job. You may have done the same thing in some company in the name of gaining experience. An obvious example of this kind is today's finance companies, which are multiplying in number. There are perhaps more financial institutions, including cooperatives, than their customers. The employees of such finance companies are the first beneficiaries, who have progressed day after day. Today they enter the institution, tomorrow they are promoted, and day after tomorrow, they found their own institution. This has been the trend in recent years.

The mentality of a worker/employee can be understood at the following points:

- He who knows nothing is not an employee.
- He who realizes his ignorance may become a general worker.
- There is one who knows, but doesn't realize his knowledge. Such a person can be employed after training or motivation.
- He is a perfect worker who knows the work and is aware of his skill.

Sometimes workers may display the following traits:

- Working lazily and being frequently absent
- Attempting to maintain self-defense
- Being unusually arrogant
- Being scared or frightened
- Tending to react quickly
- Being unnecessarily mute
- Being unsociable or introverted
- Being unclear in speech

A clever man was riding a buffalo, and his aim was to keep moving. He has given the grass through his stick. The buffalo moved for grass, but the man saved his grass too.

Workers are to be motivated and inspired in their works rather than criticized, discouraged, blamed, and punished. For motivation, the following tips are useful:

- Show respect.
- Honor the worker.
- Make the job interesting.
- Listen to the worker.
- Offer chances.

- Provide training.
- Guarantee the workers' rights.

Workers can be further motivated by telling them some success stories and sharing with them inspiring books and films. Sometimes the best thing is organizing for their welfare activity, as Reebok International does.

Reebok International Limited, a subsidiary of the German sportswear company Adidas, is a producer of athletic shoes, apparel, and accessories. It has factories in forty-five countries.

In the past, Reebok had an association with outsourcing through sweatshops, but today it claims it is committed to human rights. In April 2004, Reebok's footwear division became the first company to be accredited by the Fair Labor Association. In 2004, Reebok also became a founding member of the Fair Factories Clearinghouse, a nonprofit organization dedicated to improving worker conditions across the apparel industry.

But the workers or stakeholders should undertake self-motivating factors by themselves.

Once upon a time there was a truck driver. The owner of the truck had a hot nature, and he always gave orders harshly to his driver. The driver didn't reply, but internally he kept count. One day, he drove the truck into a very deep gorge and totally destroyed it. The owner went into bankruptcy, and the driver went to jail.

Leadership in Business

Sometimes a boss orders his staff harshly and angrily. It may help to bring positive results for that moment, but it also brings a final ending for forever too.

If we hire lazy, inactive, wage-waiting, pension-waiting employees, the work in our company won't be effective. Business is like a tree. The investors are the farmers who nurture it. If there is a defect anywhere from any party, the tree won't bloom and fruit. Then the loss will have to be borne by the investor, who in turn can't employ the workers in the company. Therefore, it is apparent that a business firm isn't set up only for the investors or proprietors; it equally exists for the advantage of the workers as well. If any worker/employee attempts to cheat the proprietor, he or she may eventually be cheating himself. Cheating takes place everywhere.

Mind refresher: *"The whole office is having a picnic for the last few days."*

"How's that?"

"Because the boss is on vacation."

Some examples of cheating include cheating on examinations, cheating of a customer by a merchant/vendor, cheating of juniors by seniors, and so on.

In the past, there was a traffic policeman nearby my house, Mustang Chowk. He was deployed there for the control and checking of vehicles, but he wasn't standing at the roundabout. He was always talking either with us or other local youths in a nearby tea shop. One day we asked him a question: "Why don't you carry out your duty sincerely by standing at the post where you need to be?" He replied, "If I stood there, every driver/vehicle owner would notice me and control themselves; nobody would violate the traffic rules. If I hide here, someone collides there or violates the rule in another way. And then I shall go and catch him." This is the mentality of a worker.

> *This traffic policeman may represent almost all the workers who are employed/hired for certain works. The policeman either wants to have some financial benefits from the drivers/vehicle owners or show his seniors his heroic deed by catching the defaulters.*

No human being is infallible. Everyone is destined to commit mistakes knowingly or unknowingly. We are guilty of mistakes almost every day. It is not necessary that we need to be noticed by someone else from outside. Our guilts or misdemeanors will suffocate ourselves. We can't believe ourselves if we commit any crime—frivolous or felony. The guilty feeling itself is a kind of mental harassment.

Once I was invited to be in a wedding by an old chum of mine. I had to buy a gift as a dowry to the bride, but as I was a little hurried, I reached the wedding spot without anything in my hand. I had to at least buy an envelope and insert some money inside it. The envelope wasn't available either. I was invited for lunch, and after I ate the lunch, I was much puzzled about what to do. I couldn't endow cash money without an envelope. During my dilemma, someone called me, and at once I left the festivity without making any gift. Sure, no one noticed me returning without gifting the bride, but even today, I have a guilty feeling at least when I see that chum of mine. Though he doesn't have any suspicion of that kind regarding me, I get frightened myself. I think this is the worst punishment in the world.

Others may not notice our guilt or crime. The physical punishment (it may be a penalty of a sum or imprisonment) may last only one day, but the inward confession of crime, though the scoundrel isn't punished, will be lifelong. An innocent person can go to jail for five years, but at least he has a mental satisfaction that he hasn't committed any crime. He is innocent and remains gratified forever. On the contrary, the guilty man who is not punished is always consumed by suspicion, doubting himself, suffering nervousness and mental terror. Mental torture is worse than physical torture. Lying to others is exactly lying to oneself. Mental peace is the most sought element today.

So far as peace is concerned, let's talk about Gautam Buddha, who advocated peace 2,500 years ago. If peace were the ultimate goal of the world, it might have been established in 2,500 years. Peace is not an absolute element. Peace has great value today because we haven't got peace. If the world were peaceful, nobody would chant the world "peace" from time to time. Mental peace is just a feeling. Bin Laden might have felt "peace" in killing other people. We human beings are always crazy about things that we haven't got. Helen Keller said, *"It is human nature to appreciate little what they have and long for the things they haven't."*

When I was in Lumbini, I valued the significance of peace, and I found that the whole area of Lumbini was echoing with peace. There were inscriptions everywhere. At the main entrance of Lumbini, on a slate, there was an inscription focusing on the five principles of cooperation and peaceful coexistence. I read them, and even today, I remember the five principles:

- Nonviolence
- Not stealing
- Not lying
- No adulteration
- No conceit/vanity

Mind refresher: *Before leaving to go abroad, a businessman asked his legal advisor to send him a fax regarding his case pending in the court when a decision was made.*

A week later, the lawyer sent him a fax reading, "Truth has been rewarded."

The businessman faxed back, "File an appeal against it."

Customers

As we know, customers are the bold marker pen in a business pen set. A very famous Indian business caste, the "Marwadi," used to say:

The shop is my temple.
Commodity is grace.
The customer is god, and
I am the priest.

Customers are regarded as gods by some people. They are donators or guests. In other words, they are the paying guests. There are two general types of customers—permanent and temporary. Permanent customers are the ones who frequently purchase goods from the same shop or consume the products of a company on a regular schedule. Temporary customers are different. They visit a shop or company without any prior notice in a sudden way. You can't estimate anything from temporary customers.

Today there are new concepts in business. Customers are also interested in investing money. The distance between the promoters/investors and customers is slowly being deleted. If any public company issues its general public shares, there are crowds to purchase them. This indicates that a customer wants to be an investor as well.

Network businesses and cooperatives are examples of this kind. In the past, customers were for merchants only; this concept has changed today. Customers are ready to play the twofold roles of both customer and investor.

The term "business family" comprises three members—investors, workers, and customers. All of them are supposed to carry out their own responsibilities. The investors/proprietors/producers need to produce and sell quality goods, which are required to satisfy the needs of the customers. The workers need to be sincere to the producer or the company. Only faithful and honest workers can assist in propelling a business ahead. Customers may fulfill their duty by identifying quality products, hygienic goods, and beneficial commodities. This will eventually encourage the genuine and sincere entrepreneurs, and the maximum amount of profit can be a core motto of each businessperson.

My friend used to buy commodities in a big shop over seven years. In my calculation, he had spent more than 100 millon in that shop already, and they had a good relationship too. Things changed, however. He had financial difficulties, and there still remained a 20,000 debt from the past six months in that shop. He wanted to pay, but the shopkeeper, who was his friend before, used to ask him for payment in a very rude manner. My friend paid but he never has returned to that shop even though now he has good financial resources that he uses to buy more than that quantity.

The debt of twenty thousand was only 0.02 percent of the total of his earlier purchases. Even if he didn't pay such a small percentage, the owner would not suffer any loss, because he had already earned more from his past purchases. When my friend paid, the owner received the 0.02 percent but lost out on future revenue forever.

A customer is part of the business family. A good business leader believes in "exchange thought" and never expects only business from customers. A small percentage of bad debts never affects the business, and posting a little bad debt is better than treating one's customers with anger. A businessman should always help a customer when he is in difficulties; that will create permanent business for the long term.

When we talk about leadership, we may think that leadership actually presents in politics. But leadership sustains in all places—from politics to a poultry firm, from the family to famous organizations, or from a school to a sophisticated business organization. Wherever leadership is, its nature may be the same—leading others. A business leader is devoted to promoting his or her business. A leader in an office leads the staff and the total office affairs. Even the leader in a family has to lead the family well.

In business, efficiency in leadership is associated with the success of the company. Especially in the leadership training season, we use an old and gold text: the general differences between a boss and a leader are to be as follows:

Boss	**Leader**
A boss creates fear. *Causes* -He just wants to gain but doesn't know how to gain. -He wants prompt returns. -He wants profit only to him. -He doesn't want to share his ideas.	A leader creates confidence. *Causes* -He believes his success depends only on others' assurance. -He believes that confidence is the key to success
A boss creates resentment. *Causes* -He believes that commanding creates gain.	A leader promotes enthusiasm. *Causes* -He believes that enthusiasm makes self-motivation.

A boss says "I."	A leader says "We."
Causes	**_Causes_**
-He wants to be superior.	-He loves to share the credit.
-He feels that the result is achieved due to his own reason.	-He believes that group effort can achieve the goal.
A boss only blames.	A leader looks at mistakes.
Causes	**_Causes_**
-He always sees that mistakes are made by others.	-He knows mistakes can be corrected.
-He can't control his arrogance.	-He realizes that mistakes may take place while working.
A boss knows how.	A leader shows how.
Causes	**_Causes_**
-He feels he knows everything.	-He thinks that sharing with others makes things easier for the future.
A boss makes work drudgery.	A leader makes work interesting.
Causes	**_Causes_**
-He doesn't know the proper way.	-He believes that when a worker enjoys his work, it is easy to achieve the goal.
A boss relies on authority.	A leader relies on cooperation.
Causes	**_Causes_**
-He doesn't want to share ideas and activity with his staff.	-He believes in helping to achieve the goal.
A boss drives.	A leader leads.
Causes	**_Causes_**
-He doesn't want to do hard work himself.	-He wants to work himself in a proper way.

Words have power. Sweetly uttered words may maintain good relationships. Not only the owner but also the workers have a care and love of the company. No worker wants his company to fail. The leadership needs to know this reality and motivate the workers for better performance. A machine requires timely maintenance and servicing; in the same way, a worker needs to be motivated from time to time. The leadership is to lead the company representing all the human resources of the company. The words "I" and "me" or "my" may irritate other workers. The company is thriving due to "our" joint efforts. This is "our" company, all of "us" are equally responsible for the success of the company, and so on. These are the utterances to be used by the leadership.

Leadership Ideas from an Ancient Era

If your popularity and products reach worldwide, it is quite significant for the pinnacle of success. Many elements like communication, marketing, transportation, and so on are helpful to gain such a goal. But an interesting, curious, and obvious example of this is that when Buddha was born 2,500 years ago, such aspects of business as communication, transportation, and marketing were not very well developed in comparison with the situation nowadays. How could Lord Buddha and his disciples be successful in spreading Buddhism worldwide?

- How was he enlightened? (Like producing commodities)
- What was his leadership role? (How to build a team and make it work)
- How did that spread worldwide? (Way of marketing)

Here I would like to talk especially about his leadership role so it may assist us more in our enterprises.

How Buddha was Enlightened

We may assume that Buddha used his five principles (nonviolence, no stealing, no lying, no adulteration, and no conceit/vanity) in producing his commodities. Such principles can help a struggling businessman reach success.

Buddha first studied with famous religious teachers of the day and mastered the meditative achievements they taught. But he found that they did not provide a permanent end to suffering, so he continued his mission. He next attempted an extreme severity, which was a religious search common among the Shramanas, a religious culture different from the Vedic one. Gautam underwent prolonged fasting, breath-holding, and exposure to pain. He almost starved himself to death in the process. He realized that he had taken this kind of practice to its limit and had not put an end to suffering. So in a significant moment, he accepted milk and rice from a village girl and changed his approach. He devoted himself to anapanasati meditation, through which he discovered what Buddhists call the path of moderation between the extremes of abandon and self-shame

From this lesson, a businessman may learn the following about how to produce goods:

1. Education is essential; but if you do not excel in that, commit and go to find the next key element.

2. Very smart work and dedication are very important to produce new products.

3. Also necessary is to not produce things before they are in demand.

Leadership style of Buddha

Currently, business leadership is a very significant topic throughout the entrepreneurial world. In this area, Buddhism has its own solitary management theory and practice that has developed over a long period of time. From this section, a businessman may learn management—how to build teams and how staffs are self-motivated to reach the company's goal.

As early as Sakyamuni Buddha's time, the Sangha community had a well-developed management system. In due course, the system continued through several changes and developed stylish methods of management and leadership. In the Avatamsyka sutra, commenting on the "three refuges," Buddha said: "Taking refuge in the Sangha means one should make the Sangha a well-administered and pleasant-sounding community for all sentient beings." From this remark, it can be observed that Buddhist Sangha communities were organizations that did extremely well in managerial expertise.

When Siddhartha was enlightened, he taught the Dharma at Deer

Park to his previous followers. The five Bhiksus turned into the first Sangha group. In time, the community grew into worshippers who integrated the six groups of disciples, that is, the Bhiksus, Bhiksunis, Sraamaneras, Srameneriksunis, Upasakas, and Upasikas. Among them, about 1,250 monastics were usually at the Buddha's side. It is a thing of curiosity how Siddhartha dealt with such a huge community. Here are some of his managerial policies:

1. Democratic governing

(Much of this information comes from the website http://www.blia.org/english/publications/booklet/pages/35.htm.)

The "Karma Assembly" system was the highest authority governing monastic life. The goal of the system was to promote a democratic way of life. The Karma Assembly meetings were regularly convened on the fifteenth of each month. At these meetings, members of the assembly reviewed any violation of the precepts that occurred during the month, determined the appropriate discipline for the offender, and decided how it would be carried out. There are two types of karma cases: (1) cases involving disputes and violations, and (2) cases not involving disputes and violations. The former dealt with disputes and disagreements among monastics or violations of precepts; the latter dealt with the appropriateness of the monastics' daily behavior and their proper guidance, or the admission of a new member into the Sangha community. The Karma Assembly provided a formal and rigorous mechanism to promote fellowship, harmony, and mutual support of the Sangha community. It enabled the community to become an ideal moral society where t-embracing virtues of giving affectionate speech, beneficial deeds, and teamwork were always practiced.

2. Mutual support and responsibility

When the initial Sangha of the five Bhiksus was formed immediately after Buddha's enlightenment, the "four principles of living" were laid down to guide them toward righteous living: "Eat only food from alms," "Wear only discarded medicine," and so on. Further, the monastics were warned to shun eight evil possessions that were considered to be hindrances to their practice, that is, houses and gardens, plants, grains and crops, servants and slaves, pets and animals, money and jewels, utensils and tools, and decorated beds. As the size of the Sangha community increased and in response to the problem of the rainy season and constant requests from their benefactors, the rules were modified to allow receipt of donated clothes, food, houses, and gardens. Regardless of the summer retreat during the rainy season and throughout ordinary daily life during the rest of the year, a communal form of living was maintained. The communal rule required that except for each monastic's own clothing and bowls, all other supplies, tools, bedding, houses, and gardens were public goods, not to be individually possessed. Repair and maintenance of equipment and tools were distributed among the members in each of the Sangha residences. An elder was elected to lead the daily operation, teach the Dharma, maintain the code of conduct, and channel any speech and information delivered by Lord Buddha. Although the lifestyle changed somewhat over a period of time, all Sangha communities still followed the basic principle of an alms system, as well as sharing support and responsibilities.

3. The law is equal for all

Buddha instructed that all sentient beings have Buddha character and that all humans are naturally equal. As a result, his teaching dismantled the societal caste system prevalent at that time. He believed himself and said, "All things arise from causes and conditions, not formed by gods or God." True deliverance depends on the four Noble Truths and the Three Dharma Seals. Buddha habitually made the following comments: "I myself am just a member of the Sangha" and " I do not govern; the Dharma governs." Buddha never considered himself "Boss"; rather, he let the truth govern. The Sunhat community was ruled by the members' respect for moral conduct. Upon admission, each member had to give up his or her previous social status, wealth, fame, and other privileges, and all external classifications and differentiations were disregarded. Members differed only in stages of internal development. The operation of the Sangha community was based on mutual respect and love, and sometimes on the order of seniority. Thus, the Bhiksus, Biksunis, and others each had their own rules. When disputes arose, the Seven Reconciliation Rules made by Buddha were followed to settle the conflict.

4. Distributed Leadership

Siddhartha, as the leader of the Sangha community, led all by his teaching and by establishing the precepts for the group. He selected knowledgeable and righteous Bhiksus and Bhiksunis to be the "instructing" monastics to teach the Dharma and precepts. Among them, he selected the seniors to provide guidance, to advise, and to observe the progress of the monastics under their supervision.

5. Communication and interaction

Buddha periodically convened all members of the Sangha community on the eighth and fourteenth or fifteenth of each month to recite the precepts. Such gatherings provided an excellent opportunity for interaction among the members and a way of fostering shared values for productive and harmonious living.

6. Mutual admiration and harmony

Guided by the Dharma, the Sangha community practiced the "six points of Reverent Harmony" in communal living. They are: (1) doctrinal unity in views and explanations to ensure common views and understanding; (2) moral unity in observing the precepts to achieve equality for all under the rules; (3) economic unity in community of goods so to effect fair distribution of economic interests; (4) mental unity in belief to provide mutual support in spiritual cultivation; (5) oral unity in speech to nurture compassion and love; and (6) bodily unity in behavior to assure nonviolence and harmonious living.

MANAGEMENT ACCORDING TO BUDDHIST SUTRAS

In the twelve divisions of Buddhist trinities, discussions related to management are everywhere. Examples from two familiar sutras are illustrated below:

1. Management perspective from the Amitabha sutra

In the Amitabha sutra, the western pure land of ultimate bliss built by the Amitabha Buddha is an example and model of management excellence. In the western pure land, there are seven levels of parapets and balustrades, seven layers of curtains and networks of precious stones, seven rows of spice trees, seven-storied pavilions decorated with seven jewels, and seven lakes filled with pure water. The air vibrates with celestial harmonies. The streets are paved with gold, salve, lapis lazuli, and crystal. The trees and flowers exude delicate fragrance and spices. All these numerous decorations and adornments make it the most beautiful land. In this wonderful land, there are no traffic accidents; all traffic moves smoothly. There are no quarrels or bickering; everyone is well behaved. There is no private ownership; there is no need, given the perfect economic system. There are no crimes or victims; everyone is absolutely safe and tries to live in peace and help each other.

The Amitabha Buddha is not only an expert in ecological management, but also an expert in human resource management. He guides the spiritual development of sentient beings, teaching them to recite his name with mindfulness. Everyone in this pure land is guaranteed to never recede from his or her practice. In this land of ultimate bliss, everyone is respectful, compassionate, peaceful, and joyful.

2. Management perspective from the lotus sutra (Avalokitesvara's universal Gate chapter)

Avalokitesvara is a remarkable expert in management. He or she manages people by relieving their suffering, bestowing upon them virtues and wisdom, and satisfying all of their needs. He or she transforms himself or herself into thirty-two different identities to facilitate his or her edification of people. The chapter of universal Gate mentions that "Depending on what identity is most conducive to the deliverance of a sentient being, Avalokitesvara will transform himself/herself into that image to elucidate the Dharma." With his or her great compassion, he or she relieves people from suffering and brings them joy. A modern manager has to be equipped with Avalokitesvara's power of accommodating people's needs. He or she has to establish effective measures to solve problems in modern organizations. One can learn an enormous amount from Avalokitesvara's dedication to "responding to whoever is desperate and wherever there's danger" and "forever delivering sentient beings from the sea of suffering."

Management in the Chinese Monastery

In Chinese, the phrase "groves of trees" refers to a monastery where monastics live. It has the connotation of a place where weeds do not grow and the trees are upright due to the presence of specific rules and measures. Buddhism strongly emphasizes a congenial relationship between an individual and the group. Thus, communal rules such as the "six points of Reverent Harmony" and the "Rules of Ethic," instituted by Chan Master Bay Zhan, existed. The management of a Chinese monastery relies on principles such as self-commitment, self-monitoring, and self-discipline. The goal is to create a congruous Sangha community so that the Dharma can rule in this world permanently. The Chinese monastery thus placed its management emphasis on shared responsibility and a harmonious group relationship. The system can be summarized in the following four characteristics:

1. Government by high merit
In the monastery, all property is publicly owned. There are rules to host visiting monastics from the ten directions. In a public monastery that is open to all, the abbot is chosen externally from renowned elders of the ten directions. In a private monastery that is not open to the public, the abbot selects from internal elders who have distinguished themselves in virtue and knowledge.

2. Equality in labor
Chinese Chan monasteries rely on collective farming. The principle of equal labor is strictly followed. Everyone, regardless of rank or seniority, has to participate in fieldwork. The Chan Master Banishing set a perfect example when he insisted, "If I do not work today, I will not eat today."

3. Shared Responsibility
Led by the abbot, a monastery usually divides the responsibilities and tasks among members. Everyone has his or her own duties, with each supporting the other. The personnel assignments are categorized into a dichotomy of "administrator" versus "manual or operational," internal service versus external service.

The leader's sole goal is to serve the saga community by maintaining the harmonious order of the monastery. The Chan monastery Rules of Proper Conduct says, "The monastery exists for its members. To edify members, the elder is elected. To mentor members, the upper seat is designated. To uphold members, direction is chosen. The job of a kamadana is to maintain accord among members by distributing duties fairly. The job of a cook is to take care of members' food. A general affair administrator is installed to plan the operation for all members. A treasurer is assigned to handle financial matters. A clerk writes and maintains the record for members. A librarian keeps the Tripitaka safe for members. The receptionist welcomes guests of true members. An attendant is a messenger for members. A security guard watches clothes and bowls for members. A medicine specialist prepares medicine for members. A bathing-room host provides bathing services to members. The wood-collector is to wood up before the true approach of winter. The fire-tender is to make sure of adequate wood and charcoal for the burners, before meditation and breakfast. The alms-beggar gathers offerings from the street for members. The foremen of graders lead, and maintenance workers clean the facilities for members. Housekeepers serve members. Well-defined jobs are an important factor driving the success and growth of an organization."

4. Code of communal living

In addition to the Buddhist precepts, Chinese monasteries have developed a set of rules governing true daily operation of monastery life. For example, Master Dao An, during the Eastern Tin Dynasty, established the following three sets of rules for his followers:

- The rules for walking meditation, sitting meditation, sutra recital, and Dharma talks
- The rules for practice, dining, and daily routines, and
- The rules for task assignment, renewal of vows, and repentance.

The rules of ethics enacted by Chan master Bai Zhang during the Tang Dynasty and other rules such as those in the Chan Monastery Rules of Proper Conduct are documented evidence of monastic discipline. These well-defined codes of conduct were instrumental in the development of the songha organizations.

Executive Style in Temples

There are hundreds of temples and affiliated associations all over the world of Guang shan. Leading such a number requires the supremacy of the executive. How do Guang shan lead and manage an organization of this size? The response is always the same: "Of course, there are many ways to do it." These are four essential ideologies:

1. There are **no fixed associations between disciples and masters**; none of the Guang shan disciples are permanently affixed to any individual master. All the disciples belong to groups differentiated by the time of entry into the order, such as first generation, second generation, third generation, and so forth. Because the disciples do not follow a certain master, there is no rivalry or competition between them.

2. **No private ownership of money or funds.** No one in Guang shan is allowed to own property or accumulate savings. All the money goes to the order. Although the members do not possess money, this does not mean that funds are not available for their support. The order usually takes care of their food, clothes, travel, medicine, study abroad experiences, and visitations, including gifts for shaving their heads (to formally become monastic practitioners). As for Guang Shan, all the money belongs to the order, not the individual, but everyone enjoys comfortable support under an excellent cooperative system.

3. **Mandatory rotation of jobs and positions** following the principle that "fresh water comes only from flowing water; a rolling stone gathers no moss." No one "owns" any branch temple, worship place, or affiliated enterprises. This year one may be the abbot or abbess of a particular temple. Next year he or she may be reassigned to another temple. There are many

benefits from job rotation. Among them are opportunities for learning and growth, for interaction and networking, and for gaining additional experience.

4. **Promotion and performance evaluation system.** A member of the Guang shan order starts with the title of "purifier," progressing through "bachelor" and "practitioner" to "instructor." Advancement depends solely on each individual's effort and performance in scholarship, Dharma practice, and service to the organization. Because of this orderly system, Guang shan has enjoyed a smooth and successful growth over the years.

From the concepts above, there are lessons to take away from religion-based management techniques:

- Consider the strategic implication of the organization as a whole,
- Divide responsibilities, with well-defined job descriptions.
- Have knowledge of the importance of coordination.

How Buddhism spread worldwide

"All men are my kids, and I am like a father of them. Naturally, every father wishes the excellence and the cheerfulness of his children; I wish that all men should be happy always." These are the words of **Emperor Ashoka**, who lived 2,300 years ago. During Ashoka's grandfather's time, the Kalinga army had only 60,000 infantry, 1,000 cavalry, and 700 elephants. During Ashoka's father's time in power and at the beginning of Ashoka's reign, Kalinga must have improved its armed forces considerably. The army marched toward Kalinga. Ashoka

himself was the chief of his huge army. The Kalinga army defended against the Magadha army and fought bravely.

Ashoka won a glorious victory. But he cried, "What have I done?" True, Ashoka was victorious and Kalinga was his. What was the price of this victory? Ashoka, who led the army, saw the battlefield with his own eyes.

As far as his eye could see, he saw only the corpses of elephants and horses, and the limbs of soldiers killed in the battle. There were streams of blood. Soldiers were rolling on the ground in unbearable pain. There were orphaned children. And eagles flew about to feast on the dead bodies.

Not one or two but hundreds of terrible sights greeted Ashoka's eyes. His heart was broken with grief and shame.

He felt unhappy over the victory, which he had won at the cost of so much suffering. "What a dreadful deed have I done? I was the head of a vast empire, but I longed to subjugate a small kingdom and caused the death of thousands of soldiers; I widowed thousands of women and orphaned thousands of children." With these oppressive thoughts in his mind, he could not stay there any longer. He led his army back toward Pataliputra with a heavy heart.

Ashoka became the lord of Kalinga as he had wished. But the victory brought him not joy but grief. The sights of grim slaughter he had seen dimmed the pride of victory. Whether Ashoka was resting, sleeping, or awake, the scenes of agony and death he had seen on the battlefield haunted him at all times; he could not have peace of mind even for a moment.

Ashoka understood that the flames of war not only burn and destroy on the battlefield but spread to other fields and destroy many innocent lives.

The suffering caused by war does not end on the battlefield; it continues to poison the minds and lives of the survivors for a long time. At this time Ashoka was at the height of his power; he was the head of a vast empire; he had no equal in wealth or armed strength. And yet the Kalinga war, which was his first war, also became his last war! The power of arms bowed before the power of Dharma (righteousness).

He promised that he would never again take to arms and that he would never again commit such a crime against humanity. And it proved to be the oath of a man of iron.

In the history of the world, many kings have sworn not to fight again after they had been defeated.

But how many kings have been moved by pity in the hour of victory and laid down arms?

Perhaps there has been only one such king in the history of the whole world—Ashoka.

The victory of Dharma brings with it love

and affection. Devanampriya believes that, however small may be the love gained by its victory, it brings ample reward in the other world.

This is what Ashoka has said in one of his inscriptions.

The teaching of Buddha brought peace to Ashoka, who was haunted by memories of the agony he had seen in Kalinga.

The gloomy Ashoka was attracted to Buddha's message of peacefulness, kindness, and love of mankind. A disciple of Buddha, nane as Upagupta, brought Ashoka into Buddhism. From that day, Ashoka's heart became the home of compassion, right living, love, and nonviolence. The gloomy Ashoka gave up hunting and eating meat. He put an end to the killing of animals for the royal kitchen. Realizing that it was not enough if he lived a virtuous life, he proclaimed that all his subjects also should live a life of righteousness. He ordered statues made of the dharma chakra, the peace pillar, to place at crossroads, parks, and other major places to make walkers curious. Under his rule, religion was starting to market, and rapidly it extended worldwide.

From this text, a businessman may learn about marketing. The following are important points to be learned:

- The quality of a product can undermine marketing. If a product is inferior but sells through exaggeration, a negative

impression will be made that will result in a negative impact even for the next product.
- Publicity is very important for public awareness.
- A quality product that attains publicity automatically turns into a recommendation, which is more precious than marketing.

Conclusion About Leadership

Out of the above tips and the features of leadership, the democratic feature is regarded as the most significant one. In a democracy, everyone can speak and each one is heard. The leadership policy is determined by representing the feelings and ideas of all the participants. One demerit of democracy is that the decision-making process is a time-killing factor because many people have many ideas; including everyone's idea by compromising them is an uphill job. Furthermore, dissidents are granted the right of protest at the point where they disagree. Democracy enables people with different views to formulate many small supporting groups. This may eventually cause division within unity.

If any leadership attempts to function with absolute democracy, it may not be able to move ahead. People are also required to exhibit democratic conduct. Leaders are required to adopt the system of leadership as per the situation and circumstances. The leader can modify and change his or her policy in accordance with the situation. If the subjects are easy, peaceful, and cooperative, the leader can be democratic and flexible to the people. When the subjects are rude, stern, disruptive, and even destructive, tyrannical in nature, the leader is needed to change the behavior of the subjects.

When policies are made, they need to be beneficial to the maximum number of people. The task of policy making depends on coordination and mutuality between the parties; for it to succeed, democratic manners and attitudes are prerequisites. Formulation of laws, regulations, and policies may not be so difficult, but their implementation is quite significant and challenging. So at the point of the execution of such policies, the leadership may be required to be stern and autocratic.

It is human nature to seek what people don't have. This nature has always made humans prone to change and revolutions. The world-famous woman Helen Keller is worth quoting. "It is human nature to long for the things they haven't and appreciate little what they have." A human being is naturally a discontent creature. But this discontentment is the basis of progress and upward movement.

Each human being, whether hero or villain, has a positive aspect of thinking. The only thing is that moral and law-abiding people are comparatively more positive on matters than morally corrupt people. There are some people who are very vain and conceited, and they are likely to interpret things in their own favor only. We can test human mentality very easily from an instance: see the people going into a film hall and watch their reactions toward the heroes and villains. Almost all of the audience, whoever they are, may empathize in the pain and pleasure of the protagonists and they may curse or hate the antagonists. Isn't it enough to say that humans have positive aspects? The positivist in the human brain hasn't gone extinct.

Almost everyone, even a criminal, may favor Rama rather than Ravana, Krishna rather than Kansha. This positivity is deeply seated at the very root of the id, but when the id is governed by ego and superego at the external level due to the prevalent circumstances and shortcomings or predicaments, the positivity, while emerging out from the very internal feeling, turns to negativity and it drives people toward misdemeanors and felonies. So we are required to look into that positivity and not let it be corrupted. Positive feelings and emotions have a great role in leadership and the implementation of policies.

Governance is like a machine, and the leaders are mechanics. The people are the beneficiaries in this regard. So long as the machine works itself or the system is on a smooth run, no mechanic may be required; but when there is some problem in the machine during the operation period or at the time of its exhaustion, perhaps the system needs to be changed or the machine needs to be revamped. Efficient leadership is sought at that time.

CHAPTER NINE

Formula for Success

If there is any complicated question in the world one can ask, it is "What is the key idea to success?" I have asked that very question to some so-called successful people, but I have been unable to get a satisfactory reply from them. *A success is only a step ahead; its destination is unlimited. A person successful today may be a failure tomorrow. Our future is always uncertain, and therefore the success that we aspire to may be wandering within that uncertainty. Success is the very wish of a person.*

Here is a real story. The eight richest people of the world met in 1923 and made a list of their assets, which totaled more than the property of the American government. They had earned the property through different means, but twenty-five years later, you know what happened:

Charles Schwab went bankrupt.
Howard Hubson went insane.
Arthur Cutton died insolvent.
Richard Whitney was sent to jail.
Albert Call was pardoned in jail.
Jessie Livermore committed suicide.
Leon Fraser committed suicide.
Evar Quize committed suicide.

I already mentioned that earning and saving a lot money is not the means to succeed in business. If we follow business principles, then success comes and lasts. So here I describe the formula for success.

The Four P's: Planning, Preparation, Practice, and Presentation

So far as my conscience, study, and experience are concerned, the key elements to success are as follows: planning, preparation, practice, and presentation. I like to call them the four P's, and they were presented in the business textbook *Principles of Management*.

As we know, a ladder has several steps, and we can climb the ladder only through step-by-step walking; if we jump, we may fall. Similarly, in business, never try to jump. We should plan, prepare, practice, and then present in sequence.

Planning

The initial step is planning, which is the entry element for success. There is no success without planning. *It is also said that a good plan is half accomplishment.*

For instance, let's say we are going to build a house anywhere in Nepal. As a rule, what we do normally is that we ask an engineer to sketch a map in haste, within two or three days, and then we start building the house, with *only fifteen or twenty lakh in our bank account. It may take some eight or nine months to perhaps a year to get the house complete, and the budget also may exceed its estimation. We are likely to exceed both the time and budget projections. We may modify the structures of the house while building.*

On the contrary, westerners spend enough time in planning. It may take them six months to consult an engineer, and then they accomplish the work of building within three months.

We need to be wise and careful while making a plan on paper. It is easier and far more economical to correct things on paper while planning than to modify the structures later.

In my view, there are three stages in making a plan properly:

1. Survey
2. Analysis
3. Decision

A survey is a kind of search. One can learn a lot from the history of the past, and this knowledge can be gained through survey. Surveying is like the collection of data or materials, and thereafter you can analyze them, putting them together.

Topics of survey

Expenses

- Raw material
- Operation cost
- Direct workers
- Indirect workers
- Repair and maintenance
- Office over head
- Interest of loan
- Insurance and audit fee

Income

- sales cost of product
- other income

Analysis is the process where data are calculated and achieve the result. It is an examination that shows the fact about past and able to show assumption of future as well. You can analysis your business plan by calculating as following.

- Total capital investment (equity and loan)
- Cash flow
- Rate of return
- Break even point
- profit

Mind refresher: *A child wrote to his parents, "Dear Mom and Dad, I have not heard anything from you for the last two weeks. Please send me a check immediately so that I will know you are all right."*

After the stage of analysis, you need to make your **decision** and set your plan by identifying what is right and what is wrong. Your decision is your precise choice of right and wrong, and it is like the base camp. A mountaineer starts his journey from the base camp. Suppose you are a mountaineer in this regard. You need to build up the base camp for your success. Your decision is your commencement toward your success.

Suppose you are going to take an examination for the public service commission. You need to make a plan first. Your plan may involve: which position to apply for, what the curriculum is, where to buy the study materials, how to sit for study, and whom to consult. In this way, you need to make a top to bottom plan to successfully prepare for the examination.

Planning in business is a very sensitive matter because no business is successful without planning. Before you start your business, you need to make a survey about the potentiality of your business, the risks that may hinder you on your way, and the strategy of marketing. You need to analyze the amount of investment, the location of the business, the type of business, and so many other things before you make the foundation of your firm.

Things to be considered before opening a business include:

Leadership in Business

1. Whether the products are in demand or not
2. Whether the product or business is according to your own will and interest or not
3. The technology and raw materials required for the business
4. What banking facilities to use—or not
5. The environment and local effect of the business
6. The potential profit in your business

Then you can make a checklist of the above analysis in a table as follows, and score your business's potential for success:

Serial no.	Full mark	Score
1	500	
2	100	
3	200	
4	1000	
5	100	
6	600	
Total	2500	

If you secure a score of 50 percent or more, you are likely to start your business. In other words, the higher your score, the more likely you are to earn profit.

PREPARATION

After the planning is made, there comes preparation. *Planning is usually on paper or in the mind, whereas preparation is in action.* If you are planning to take an exam of the public service commission, now you prepare for it—you fill in the form and submit it to the respective authority, you buy the books and materials, and then you may take some instructional classes. These are your preparation. In your business, you rent a house or room, set up the interior structure, prepare to advertise and place an order for it, campaign for your business in the market, and so on. These are your preparations just before running the business.

Your plan is theoretical, whereas your preparation is the execution of the plan. While making preparation in your business, you need to consider the following:

1. Complete preparation of the financial aspect
2. Complete arrangement of technical materials
3. Orientation training for the staff
4. Execution of the marketing technique
5. Complete preparation of management

Below is a chart on which you can evaluate the results of your preparation. Evaluate each consideration and determine the result. Once the result or outcome is favorable in each category, you can move ahead toward practice, the third stage.

	Done	Undone	Result
1. Financial preparation			
2. Technical preparation			
3. Training for employees			
4. Marketing strategy			
5. Management preparation			

Practice

We know that the cheetah is said to be the fastest-running animal in nature. It can run as much as 40 km. per hour. But a record breaker in the Olympics, a human athlete, runs a 100-meter race within 9.6 seconds. In this way, the athlete runs almost as quickly as the cheetah. The human

> *being has gained on the cheetah, the fastest-running animal of nature.*

How is that possible? It is all due to practice. The old proverb says "Practice makes a man perfect." In fact, practice makes you conditioned to something. If you practice running every day or if you go on writing with your left hand, you start to feel it is easy to do so. Practice makes even impossible things plausible. Your practice is your training. A soldier always needs trainings of different types. An employee is also trained on a frequent basis. Your practice in your business means business activities of purchase and sales. If you start your business without sufficient training or practice, you may fail in your cause. You may need to modify and produce a different brand of different taste. You are required to be updated in this regard.

Presentation

This is the precious position of seeing the effect of the project. If the project is good in preparation with accurate practice but the presentation does not follow through accordingly, then you are wasting all your labor. This is very straightforward period that should be followed according to the plan. As an example, a football team may design a good plan, prepare, and practice, but if it does not follow through in presenting in the same way, it will have poor results.

In business, presentation is the vital part, so we will outline the presentation in detail:

The first day

- Right implementation of the manpower(staff) according to the plan
- Lots of advertising and publicity before opening day
- Inauguration with a special highlights program
- Outlook attraction
- Lots of attractive promotional schemes for clients
- Motivation to dealers and sub-dealers by providing lots of attraction schemes

- Quick survey on the market status

The following days

- Produce according to the market status.
- Change the negative parts.
- Continue publicity.
- Expand systematically as much as possible.
- Be sincere about cash flow and a strong accounting system

Having a formula is the key to achieving results. As an example, if we want to make water, the formula outlines the composition of hydrogen and oxygen, so we should follow the same composition. For success in business, we should follow the four P's formula to achieve our goal.

A Real Story of an Unsuccessful Businessman

A fisherman was fishing. Bread was on the hook, and both the hook and the bread were inside a clear bottle. The man wanted fish. The fish saw the bread and wanted to eat, but could not get through the bottle. There was action but no reaction, and thus no result.

Is it possible to get something without losing anything?

We may get lots of inspiration and instructions when we study a victory story, and there are lots of available texts about such stories. However, people don't care about the failure story. If we find much inspiration through success fables, we can get lots of awareness tips through unsuccessful experiences too. *A success story doesn't mean a complete motivation; it should be advised as a means of awareness from enemies. Courage on one side and awareness on the other side is the best way of accomplishing a task successfully.*

Here I will present a real story about some people with whom I had an interview. I have their permission to write it in my book on the condition that I changed their names.

Surendra (name changed) is a lovely and a really spoon-fed son of

Surya Bahadur. The priest who carried out the naming ceremony of the child pointed out that the child was very well-matched to his name. A king is said to be a lucky person when he enjoys his life without any political difficulty. Surendra's childhood life was the same as the prince of heaven. When he cried, he got food; when he smiled, he got a chance to visit his mother's lap; and when he danced, he got acknowledgment. From the above clues, we might assume that his life would never be gloomy.

Whether a prosperous person or a pauper, everyone obviously has to cross each of life's steps. Similarly Surendra also completed his childhood and became twenty-one years of age. A gorgeous lady with great luck would be his princess then.

A lady's beauty actually lies in her faith and honesty, which may refer to her chastity, and a man's success lies in his maleness, known as potency. Speaking truly, there is no need to go to parlors to get decorated with powders and flowers with dyed hairstyles. A lady remains more beautiful in her chastity and faith. Similarly a man with potency is regarded as a male.

First attraction is the beginning of love, placement into the heart is accommodating love, and being unable to break up is the madness of love. When two people of opposite sex are trapped in a love affair, there is no means of analysis. When Surendra met Ashmita, the beautiful lady, they vowed their love to each other and promised that they would never separate in their lives.

A rich man always has the motive of exposing his wealth, especially in wedding occasions. This has been a disease in Nepali ethnicity. Surya Bahadur had the same dream for his lovely son's wedding. Who was going to do the marriage? Father or son? If the son, the bride needed to be the choice of the son; but in a conformist culture, each and every choice depends on the parents.

A wealthy person always feels very powerful himself; if someone goes against his interest, he cannot understand the other's choosing freedom rather than his autocracy and he feels insulted. The same thing happened in Surendra's case. He and his bride had already gotten married, which was unacceptable in his family unit. The innocent Surendra never knew the kind of intolerable conditions that would be created by his own parents.

After his marriage, his lifestyle altered. Due to the fact that they were not accepted in the family, they rented a room and lived there. He felt very pained in this circumstance. In the past, he had a very different life at home with the parents—there were servants, a lovely family, a well-furnished garden, a bungalow, and so on. Before his marriage, he was thinking that he would need nothing besides his beloved. After his marriage, he admitted the value of money and wealth because he was now out of his home. When we live in a pond, we do not value water; but when we are in a desert, we die for water. The same thing was happening to Surendra.

Three years later, Surya Bahadur passed away, and Surendra's mother asked him to come back home and take care of the father's industries. A twenty-four-year-old young man without any commercial experience now became the chief of three industries. It is quite difficult to run a business with insufficient knowledge and experience. *A business may succeed with enormous effort and supreme commitment.* Surendra was a lad of a rich father. He never had any hard exercise in the business field. That kind of business did not match him. In the early days, he got lots of respect as the company boss; but due to his luxurious experiences, slowly he started getting frustrated in that field. He started being absent during the office hours. Employees are workers, and if they get chances, they may work lazily. These things happened in the company run by Surendra. Eventually the company went into loss, and Surendra had to borrow money to maintain the expenditures.

Surendra was in deep debt. There was no way to pay back the loan. He wished to escape from this business, but not so trouble-free to run away. Running away from his business was like catching a bear's ear for Surendra. If he freed his hands, the bear would bite him; if not, how long had he to catch the ear?

About this time, real estate was a booming business, and many of his colleagues had lots of turnover. He analyzed the situation and jumped into that new business. But it also proved very harmful to him. A dhukuti system was a society cooperative system in his culture, and he started to manage this new idea. Now he became the owner of five companies, but the turnover of all his business depended only on the part of others' money (the loan).

Now he is at the age of forty-eight, and his lovely wife is forty-six. She has had some health problems regarding her heart.

On September 21, 1990, it was sunny and the time was early evening, just as the sun was setting. Surendra sought his dinner with meat and ordered his wife to cook. Around nine o'clock after dinner, his wife felt uneasy in respiration and got a lot of sweat in the face, her respiratory system was in distress, and she felt faint. Immediately he informed his son and took her to the hospital, but the doctor declared that she had passed away forever. It was all very intolerable to Surendra.

In previous days, there had been the tension of his office, but now there were additional stresses about his family too. The days ware passing. His relatives pressured him about his next marriage. Surendra said, "In the early days I refused, but finally I also considered the necessity and then I married again."

He was forty-nine years old, but she was only twenty-six and from the countryside. She was from a poor family background, but that was not a concern for Surendra. He had to marry her for his family's support and maintenance. Unfortunately, this marriage was different from the previous one. It was a marriage to fulfill certain needs—Surendra required a wife, and the woman needed someone who could at least feed her well. They weren't married because they wanted to put their emotions and feelings together.

Due to more difficulties, his business again faced more disputes, and he couldn't control the loan. He was bankrupt, and all the rest of his property was also given to the public financier. A gloomy time came. His life had gone from alpine to grassroot, and now he had no property at all.

There was a lack of household groceries, and his wife became angry with him as she mostly needed food to eat. She usually shouted at him and even insulted him. One day, she went to her mother's house and did not come back. Later he found that she had gone abroad with a foreigner. She never came back, never came back again.

There is a proverb "If you have no money, your wife becomes your first enemy. If you don't give food to your dog, one day he bites you." The same thing applied in Surendra's life. He was an honest person himself, but nowadays people shock him without reason.

There are many Surendras in society, from whom we can take a lot of knowledge and awareness.

Enemies of Business

According to Surendra, these are the factors that constantly played a harmful role in his business. He noticed them as enemies of business:

1. Unskilled about office management
2. More trust in others than appropriate
3. Work decisions made after hasty analysis
4. Office income spent on personal life
5. Lack of seriousness
6. Many businesses at the same time
7. Lack of family support
8. Unnecessarily aggressive
9. Uncontrolled loan

Especially in developing countries like Nepal, there are lots of publicly founded businesses without any managerial proficiency and there is no focal concretion for management. In general, we may imagine an office means at least one small room with some helpers and staff, but the amount for office expenditure depends on the size of the firm. *A business is a liability of both money and honor. But within a short time, we may not get both things at once.* Sometimes we refuse some necessary items in order to control expenditures. In order to control salaries, we don't recruit an accountant; but due to the lack of a proper accounting system, you might be losing a big amount. The same thing happened in Surendra's office, so he said this factor was an opponent of his business.

There is a Hungarian proverb "The believer is happy; the doubter is wise." In fact, we may be happy when we believe others, but it is our wisdom to feel doubt about others. Once in a meeting with the past governor of the Nepal

National Bank, Ganesh Bahadur Thapa, he suggested that, "all men are thieving at chances." I have had the same experience in the business field. *If we don't trust others, there are problems running the business—and if we do trust them, therein lies the problem.* So it is one of the enemies of business, and it may be eradicated only through officials and professionals. Be an official and professional. For example, if you lend someone some money, you should get their signature with a date and return commitment in writing. Otherwise, that may be the beginning of a quandary.

A hasty decision after short examination is very destructive in the business field. After others' achievement, many copycat entrepreneurs start to open businesses without any analysis with the hope to be victorious. Beginning without data review, only by self-decision, short analysis may be a great problem in a trade.

Business is your lover. It needs your care, love, commitment, sacrifice, dedication, and proper analysis. If we are not serious in the above matters, problems enter our company and solutions go away.

A man who cannot walk may not try to run, but if can run, he may try to add further speed. We all know the story about a little child who wants to put his full hand of peanuts through a narrow-necked pot. He was unable to take them out due to expecting too much at once. Similarly if we do uncontrolled business in the greed for more profit, that may prove a great risk and eventually harm us.

A house is a kind of break and relief from all the stresses of the workday. If there is any additional stress in the house, then where can you go for relief? There is no place. A business person may have lots of stresses during the workday, and the circumstances may make him gloomy and exhausted. When he returns home, his family members don't understand the stresses he is undergoing. If he shares about some problem, he gets blamed by his family. There is no need for giant support from his family in the business, but just providing ordinary help is a key motive for his progress.

A partner means joining with another to make progress, and partners have to reduce unnecessary distrust between them. If a crisis occurs, they too frequently run for their own well-being. This is the prime cause for sinking a business.

In the early days of his business, Surendra felt his business as a fashionable desire, but later he started an uncontrolled business for earning more money. This kind of unnecessary aggression was one of the enemies he listed against his development. He calculated a loan as having fixed interest with the rest profit for him, so he took the biggest available loan, thinking he could earn through that loan. But one day he realized that loan had eaten his company.

From the above story, we may analyze that a successful business is not a matter of either the son of a rich person or a baby-style attitude. It needs lots of leading effort to truly bring about the accomplishment.

Conclusion

Aiming to gain one's wealth through business is a fashionable medium for a new generation nowadays. It is a good thought, but we need to have the have right leadership ability to succeed. We can imagine that lots of ideas, effort, commitment, and sacrifice are the basics for a business leader.

Please remember that business is not your hobby—it is your responsibility. First fall in love with your business; everything starts here.

Success is the implementation of perfect knowledge. Such knowledge comes in one of two ways: (1) from our own experience or (2) from others' experience. We can take much knowledge from own experiences that may help us after things happen, but the knowledge that we gain from others is better because it may help us *before* things happen. Books are one of the easiest, most comfortable sources from which we can gain the knowledge imparted by other people. I am confident that *Leadership in Business* is one such book.

Knowledge Is Not a Power

People say that" knowledge is a power". But it is not a factual at all. Suppose as a case, if you say a smoker person about smoke is injurious to health, if this knowledge having power he should avoid smoking recently, but he want but cant. Only few smokers can avoid it who has strong will power. So we may say "knowledge is not a power it is information only, Will power is a power and that generative by spiritual practice only." Each individual essential to Generating will power that is very important to be in action after the knowledge gaining. This book is a kind of knowledge and it may not be modify your business profession but it is sure it is the correct information, so I again share you some ideas to improve will power through spiritual practice that sequence need to be in action.

Start good tomorrow by Today- Go bed before 10 pm. - As we already discussed we need 8 hour for sleeping and should be wake up with sufficient sleep before sunrise. Please go bed before 10 pm to start right tomorrow.

Wake up 35 minute before Sunrise- We all are survived by oxygen and there in the earth as minimum 4% in afternoon and it grow up to 74 % before sun rise. See the effect of plant grow in fresh air so you will be same by this practice.

Take 3 Baths – Air bath/Water bath/Sun bath-Bathing means making fresh that increase enthused. Air bath means being in fresh air that makes freshness in your internal body ,water bath is showering that makes freshness in outer body and sun bath is being in sun side that add you addition vitamin for your required body.

Practice Meditation- Meditation is not any kind of worship it is a management practice become to positive and cautious. Be in silence place and do the meditation for positive thought and yourself.

Read Religious Book-Religious books are always in positive thought and inspiration, all kind of religious book are written with ancient research. Reading and believing with this help to put in being spiritual.

Listening Preach- preach is the source of motivation for true life. Listening preach practice affix energy in the mind that helps a man turn in to spiritualism.

Believe in Soul- There is one supreme power that we may not be seen. You may feel that is the symbol of god. This god is power of the earth, Believing with this soul helps a person to be spiritual.

Eat Balance Food- Food are categorized in three kind; Tamasik, Rajasik,. Swatik. Tamasik are those food which is known as Vegetarian, Rajasik food known as non vegetarian, alcoholic and oily, Swatik food means simple food where even garlic, onion, oily,alchol are not included. This food control a person's unnecessary emotion. Eat balance food in right time that adds more will power in your mind. Breakfast is compulsory and Dinner should be taken before 7 pm.

www.ingramcontent.com/pod-product-compliance
Lightning Source LLC
Chambersburg PA
CBHW030800180526
45163CB00003B/1101